designing contemporary congregations

designing contemporary
congregations

STRATEGIES TO ATTRACT THOSE UNDER FIFTY

Laurene Beth Bowers

THE PILGRIM PRESS

CLEVELAND

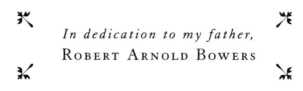

In dedication to my father,
ROBERT ARNOLD BOWERS

The Pilgrim Press, 700 Prospect Avenue, Cleveland, Ohio 44115-1100
thepilgrimpress.com
© 2008 by Laurene Beth Bowers

Scripture quotations, unless otherwise noted, are from the New Revised Standard Version of the Bible, © 1989 by the Division of Christian Education of the National Council of Churches of Christ in the United States of America and are used by permission. Changes have been made for inclusivity.

13   12   11   10   09   08   5   4   3   2   1

Library of Congress Cataloging-in-Publication Data

Bowers, Laurene Beth, 1958–
    Designing contemporary congregations : strategies to attract those under fifty / Laurene Beth Bowers.
       p. cm.
    Includes bibliographical references.
    ISBN 978-0-8298-1789-8 (alk. paper)
    1. Church growth.   2. Postmodernism—Religious aspects—Christianity.
I. Title.
BV652.25.B69 2007
254'.5—dc22   2007045236

CONTENTS

p r e f a c e

As I walked onto the beach, a friend of mine stood up to greet me saying, "Thank you for the beautiful quilt! But you are not going to believe what happened. . . ." Her husband had died of cancer in his thirties, leaving her with two small children. As a wedding gift, she had made him a quilt, but she had not sown the seam allowances to leave room for natural stretching in the wash and so the seams were splitting apart. She had asked me if I would fix the quilt for her. This was nearly two years ago and I was embarrassed that I had not gotten around to making the repairs. During the writing of this book, to take a break, I had picked up the quilt and begun working on it. After a few weeks, I finished it and brought it over to her home. As she tells the story, she had just terminated with her grief therapist feeling that it was time to move forward. When she arrived home, there was the quilt lying on a white wicker chair on her cottage porch.

What I hadn't anticipated was that her story would be part of my story. When I had first inspected the quilt, I realized that this was no small favor. To take apart a quilt and tear out all its seams in order to sew them all back together is more effort than to make a quilt from start. It would have been easier if she had handed me all new fabric and asked me to make her a brand-new quilt.

Likewise, it may be easier to design a contemporary congregation by beginning from scratch with new parishioners rather than trying to change the "old" ones. But that is not what I felt God calling me to do. Even outdated fabric can have its place in the contemporary landscape. After all, contemporary fabric will in time become outdated, and if we do not preserve antique quilts we will have lost our "chain of memory" with our past. (Antique quilts are more valuable to collectors.) With time, new congregations will either need to establish traditional foundations upon which to root themselves in history or they will fade away. Contemporizing traditional congregations, by blending traditional and contemporary features, is an evolutionary process for organized religion. My intention in this book is not to suggest that we replace traditional quilts with contemporary ones, but that we learn how to weave traditional and contemporary patterns of functioning into a vital congregation.

Currently, the movement toward designing contemporary congregations is to begin at the beginning and see what emerges. The traditional congregation is viewed as beyond hope that they will change enough to be receptive to contemporary trends. And yet, throughout history, it has been the tradition of organized religion to be responsive to contemporary trends. I suggest we revive this tradition.

Stephen C. Compton, in *Rekindling the Mainline*, speculates that the traditional church itself goes through a life cycle, emerging at birth and attaining a phase he refers to as "equilibrium."[1] In this phase, the church remains at a relatively fixated state. Just as we often assume that adults do not grow—intellectually, spiritually, or emotionally—the church seems to have reached a similar phase of life. This line of thinking has led some authors to propose that the church has to die to be resurrected, but we'd better leave the possibilities of resurrection to divine intervention, not strategies designed by humans. What most church growth specialists agree on is that the older the church, the harder it is for the congregation to grow.

As traditional churches dot the skyline, it seems more environmentally friendly to recycle the materials we already have, rather than to plant new ones. Traditional churches have historic roots that often go deep into a community. Like the roots of an established plant, they may need more nourishment than they are currently receiving. New churches may be likely to grow quickly in fertile ground, but because they have no established roots may have nothing to depend on when a dry spell comes, when their energy is depleted. For this reason, I will concentrate on renewing and reenergizing the traditional, mainline church with the hope that we can breathe new life into dry bones.

Seminaries train pastors to serve churches fifty years in the future. The problem is that most churches function fifty years in the past. Most of us, right out of seminary, experienced culture shock in the parish because there is a one-hundred-year gap between what we thought we were going to be doing as pastors and the congregation's expectations. That one-hundred-year gap stifles creativity and remolds pastors into what we think the church wants us to be. As natural people-pleasers we have sacrificed our ability to influence needed change at the expense of making a good impression. It seems so much easier to dwell snugly at ease in Zion, dishonest to our calling and clinging blindly to the traditional modes of functioning held by our foremothers and forefathers to be sacrosanct.

Somewhere along my own pilgrimage of transformation, I came across the designs of church growth specialists. First of all, let me admit, church growth is *not* my specialty. I tend to resist any agenda that is meant to collect people, like marbles, so that I can claim to serve a "bigger" church than my colleagues. Nothing aggravates me more at collegial gatherings than when a comparison is made ("How big is yours?") to determine status and relational hierarchies. People often ask me, a woman pastor, "Are you the pastor of the whole church?" and I want to answer, "No, I divide them into ones and twos, and I minister only to the twos," but such sarcasm would get me nowhere. (They are asking me if I am the associate pastor.)

I have found that many of the church growth specialists are moving away from playing the numbers game and moving toward "spiritual growth" instead. Most who write about church growth write from the perspective of the evangelical or post-evangelical church and only a select few write for the liberal church, whatever that might truly be. Whereas others seek to "transform secular space into sacred space," this approach seeks to witness to the ways that secular space has already been made sacred space through divine creation and not through our efforts. There is also a presumption in some circles that God has already decided which churches will grow and which will die; thus there is nothing that we can do to reverse the current trends of decline, nor that we should do to prevent the death of these churches. I disagree. I believe that God is sending prophets to warn us against letting this happen and encouraging us to turn around the decline with spiritual growth, which will subsequently produce numerical growth.

What is unique, then, about this book, which, even in its subtitle, "strategies to attract those under fifty," suggests yet one more book on church growth? As Michael Jinkins observers, "The literature on the church's decline seems to be the only thing growing in North American Protestantism."[2] First of all, there are very few books written by women on this subject. The large megachurches are served almost exclusively by white men. I write as a woman pastor. I also write as a practicing pastor, someone who has designed strategies based on my own experience in the local congregation. Even if the strategies presented in this book are not a custom fit for another congregation, my intention is to lift up the issues involved. I hope and pray that my story will intersect with the reader's story and that together we can witness to the work of the Holy Spirit weaving the web of salvation history as it continues to unfold.

If you are looking for a strategy to attract people for the sake of having a numerically large church, then I suggest that you read a book on how to be more entertaining. This is not a book that seeks to be flashy or to suggest glitzy techniques to attract people to organized religion. I will not speak of "seekers" or the "unchurched" because that creates a boundary between those who are in the dominant group and those who are among the marginalized, and it is debated on which side the church is currently positioned. Our church is Christ-oriented and Spirit-driven. We believe that the life of Jesus, when followed, sets a path for the rest of us to feel "happy" in this lifetime and that sharing that good news energizes us through the Holy Spirit. We seek to produce a community that emphasizes the process of spiritual transformation.

The process of writing this book itself has also been transformational. Writing is a process by which the writer changes their way of thinking as we begin looking at things in a new light. I have endeavored to produce a work that reflects my current thinking about these present-day issues and is an extension of the conversation about multiculturalism in *Becoming a Multicultural Church* (Cleveland: Pilgrim Press, 2006). In the following pages, I narrow the subject of multiculturalism with respect to age. Yet, when I speak of "postmodern" I refer to all who are "in touch" with contemporary trends, regardless of age.

While proper English syntax does not yet conform to inclusive language, I have chosen the form of using the singular noun with a plural pronoun. The he/she approach is outdated and cumbersome. The content of language in this book must reflect the process of contemporizing, and therefore I have made every attempt to present what I have to say using a postmodern literary style. Because reading time is often limited among all the tasks required of pastors who are generalists, I have kept illustrations to a minimum and employed them when a concept seems convoluted and needs further explanation to be usable. Instead of a theoretical discussion of why a strategy works, I have focused on how it relates to practice. My intention is to be practical rather than theoretical so that the reader has something to work with after reading the book.

I wish to thank everyone at The Pilgrim Press for their words of encouragement and affirmation. I thank the administrative assistant at the church I serve, Ruth Olson, whose support over the past ten years has meant so much to me. Thanks to my family, my husband Kent, and our three postmodern children, Christian, Kyle and Kelyne, who inspire me every day to reach out to attract their generation to become involved in organized religion.

introduction

For the times they are a-changin'.

BOB DYLAN

I know of few people who attend church anymore. Those outside the walls of organized religion view the church as an outdated institution, out of touch with its cultural environment, a segregated organization clinging blindly to the past and resistant to contemporary megashifts. Those inside the walls of organized religion feel frustrated that outsiders casually use the church only when they need something, for example, the ritual of baptism. They romanticize the church's glory days when young people were well represented and respected the traditions of their beloved institution. Somewhere in the middle is the painful reality that if organized religion were to gasp its last dying breath, most people couldn't care less.[1]

It is no longer "in" to attend a religious organization in the same way as it was for our parents' and grandparents' generations. The generation who became adults during the Second World War not only attended a faith community, but exhibited a high level of commitment to that organization, both in terms of participation and financial support. I will therefore refer to this generation as "the modern worshiper."

The modern worshiper attends church on a regular basis. Their moral compass points in the direction of religion and its organization as a guide for daily living. They are loyal to a specific religious organization as well as its umbrella organization or its denominational affiliation. This sense of loyalty comes from the emotional support they received during and after a personal crisis. They might say, "I could not have gotten through it without the prayers and support of my church family." Loyalty to the institution is demonstrated by sustaining its status quo, honoring tradition, and investing energy into the establishment. The modern worshiper assumes that those who do not go to church are either apathetic or atheist.

The postmodern generation, the generation succeeding that of the modern worshiper, is technologically in tune, computer literate, environmentally conscious, and an advocate for multiculturalism. Being raised by a generation who grew up in the 1960s (the early postmodern generation) and who questioned anything that reeked of "organized," the postmodern generation tends to be suspicious of the church's evangelism. They may say, "The church just wants my money." This generation is interested in religion, but calls it "spirituality" to distinguish it from the religion that is preached by an authority figure within a religious organization. They prefer to dialogue about religious questions in an Internet café, while sipping designer coffee and eating organic substances. What they believe about religion and God, they believe with the same passion as the modern worshiper. The postmodern generation, then, is just as "religious" as the modern worshiper, with the major difference being that religion for the postmodern believer is an internal process that can be practiced anywhere, while the modern worshiper perceives religion as a collective practice within the walls of organized religion.

Although dividing contemporary culture into two distinct generations may be a sweeping generalization (age is not always a reliable predictor of how someone thinks or feels about organized religion), its purpose is to understand the perspective of those who attend church and those who do not. My intention is to discern if both groups can peacefully co-exist within the same faith community, especially given that neither group has shown much interest in resolving this division. The "problem child" should not be identified as generational, as if "all our problems would be solved if every postmodern believer woke up tomorrow, saw the light, and attended a local church." The root problems in organized religion run deeper: their dynamics emerge on the surface and their ramifications have a severe impact on congregational functioning. And yet, that the next generation of believers shows little interest in organized religion *is* problematic for those who care about the future of the church.

As adjunct professor of World Religions at Quincy College, my job is to dialogue, and even debate, religion with the postmodern generation. Very few of my students are affiliated with organized religion, but most of them have an abiding curiosity for everything religious. Some fear organized religion is something toxic: that it is a brainwashing of sorts that justifies violence and war and that functions as a vehicle for oppression. The students are eager to learn something about every global religion and its practices. Western-born students are most intrigued by Eastern practices of religion, for example, Zen Buddhism, and Eastern-born students are curious about Western practices. (Quincy College is one of the most multicultural educational institutions in the Boston area, with 52 percent of its student body either recent immigrants or in America on an educational visa.)

As senior pastor of First Congregational Church in Randolph, Massachusetts, I also stand within the circle of organized religion. The members of my congregation are the people with whom I have prayed, laughed, cried, and celebrated throughout my adult life. The faces have changed, not only because I have served four churches, but through the natural ebb and flow of people going in and out of the congregation during life's transitions. I have the best interests of modern worshipers at heart. They are people I love and care about, but they are also a stubborn and stagnant people who have sacrificed for too long at the altar of "everything must stay the same" and who need gentle encouragement and caring confrontation by passionate leaders who will love them enough not to let them remain there.

CHALLENGING THE VIEWS FROM INSIDE

Within the walls of organized religion, there are three misperceptions about those on the outside: 1) they are not religious, 2) this is why they do not attend church, and 3) if the organization were to change, they would still not come. These misperceptions enable the modern worshiper to remain comfortably at ease. They conclude, "If young people are not religious and don't want to be, then why should we do anything to change for them? We might change something and not like it and then start losing the few people we have left!"

In my conversations with the postmodern believer, I have come to understand that everyone believes in *something* whether or not they attend a faith community. I used to think when one of my students professed to be an "atheist" that this meant that they did not believe in a supernatural world. But they are articulating that what they believe does not neatly fit into the prefabricated mold of a specific global religion. In other words, they may believe in a personal god but practice yoga, or they may not believe in one personal god but in many gods that control the forces of our existence. They may believe the core beliefs of Christianity but find that the spiritual practices of Buddhism help them to best express those beliefs.

It is also just as unlikely that those within organized religion would answer theological questions (about God, heaven, death, evil, and the like) in the same or even similar ways. Organized religion functions on the misperception that specific faith communities are either liberal or conservative, mainline or evangelical, post-liberal or post-evangelical, practicing or emerging. While each faith community may lean toward one side of the continuum more than the other side, the reality is that individual parishioners have different answers to theological questions, have diverse opinions about the church's relationship to its cultural environment, and vote for different political candidates whom they believe will help us resolve our justice issues. The spectrum of religious diversity encompasses a wide range of what the people who sit in the pews really believe versus what they think they should believe.

The word "religious" comes from the Latin *religio*, which means "to tie" or "to connect." Being religious means to have a connection to the divine or sacred world, in whatever form one images that numinous and awesome presence. The new age movement uses the word "spiritual" to refer to those who are not interested in organized religion and the word "religious" to refer to those with an affiliation to organized religion. Some people say they are "spiritual" who have had a negative experience in relation to organized religion. But "spiritual" refers to the process of making this connection Once the connection has been made, "spiritual" becomes "religious." One becomes religious through spiritual practices, whether through yoga, meditation, Bible study, and/or worshiping in organized religion. "Spiritual" refers to the formation of a religious connection with God, and that connection activates energy.

WHY A NEW DESIGN? (and what's wrong with the old one?)

Since the mass exodus from organized religion over the past thirty years, most congregations are realizing that to continue doing things the way we have always done them means certain death for the body of Christ. Some believe that the death of the church will allow divine intervention to resurrect it. Others believe that God needs us to prevent its death. Some churches have already died and had to close their doors because they no longer had enough money to support pastoral leadership or because they buried the fifteen little old ladies who faithfully attended every week. Sacred buildings are being converted to lovely condominiums. One way or another, houses of worship will become contemporary, either as thriving places of worship or as residential condominiums. One way or another, change is inevitable. We can either control that change or we can let that change control us. Just imagine ourselves helplessly standing on the pavement of our beloved church while the builders take down the steeple and erect a copper copula in its place. I would rather control what is happening and act as an instrument to allow God to work through me to contemporize the church and prevent its death.

During the Vietnam War in the 1960s and 1970s, churches thrived numerically and financially.[2] Such positive reinforcement confirmed the modern worshiper's perception that the way in which they functioned as a congregation was "the right way." These traditions that were embraced during this time worked because they were congruent with contemporary culture. But as culture changed, the church held even tighter to the same traditions with the hope of re-creating the glory days. "But we're not doing anything differently than we did in the glory days!" the modern worshiper laments. "Why are people not coming any more?"

As creatures of habit, we tend to repeat patterns of behavior that give us positive affirmation and help us to attain our goals. B. F. Skinner studied this phenomenon with pigeons. When the pigeons pecked on a gadget that released food, he found that this increased the likelihood that they would peck on it again. This is known as "behavioral conditioning." When the food was withdrawn (the positive reinforcement), one would expect that the behavior would cease. But surprisingly, Skinner observed that just the opposite happened. The pecking behavior actually increased with even more vigor than before.

Even when no food came out of the dispenser, the pigeons continued to do things the way they had always done them even if the desired results were no longer attained.

The design of the glory days worked because it was congruent with contemporary culture and addressed issues related to the civil rights movement, the Vietnam War, the sexual revolution, and so on. The church was the happening place in town. It attracted the younger generation and so the way they functioned as a congregation was affirmed (behavioral conditioning). But while the cultural environment progressed, the modern worshiper continued to function the same way and grew increasingly frustrated as they began to realize that they were not getting the same results. The positive reinforcement of attracting the younger generation had been withdrawn. Instead of shifting approaches, the church continued to do things the way that it had always done them, with even more conviction, and became even more frustrated.

It is often observed that the world has changed more rapidly and dramatically in the past fifty years than in the entire preceding history of humanity. Concurrently, organized religion has become overwhelmed by trying to keep up and is lagging further and further behind. Whereas our communities, neighborhoods, and worldview are shifting to embody multicultural environments, the church remains segregated. In coffee shops, health clubs, spiritual centers, and college campuses, the postmodern believer is intrigued by religious questions and learning new-age spiritual practices that are convenient and readily accessible in a culture of multitasking. The church offers one service per week at a specific location. Personal religious experience has low status in organized religion, but high status in a culture that embraces individualism. The church has a hierarchical structure that dictates that the elite at the top have the right answers to be passed to those below. Essentially, culture has designed contemporary spiritual practices in response to organized religion's inability to interact with culture.

THE POINT OF CRISIS

When a crisis arises, individuals tend to look back to the glory days, to a period of time when they were not experiencing anxiety. This looking back is a regressive pull toward functioning "the way we used to do things." Often in a time of great anxiety, this backward view is a skewed memory of what those days were actually like and they are romanticized, re-created so to speak, to be remembered more comfortably than they were experienced at the time. When parishioners experience a crisis, their anxiety naturally rises, and on instinct they recall the glory days with such fondness that they idealize the past. I used to have a cartoon over my desk with a pastor at the pulpit, and behind the pulpit is a huge portrait of the previous pastor with the caption reading, "The Greatest Pastor a Church Ever Had." Its hard to compete with such a memory, but the memory is often not based in reality; it is based on the state of high comfort, low anxiety.

It's hard to admit when we have a problem because then we have to make a change in the way we do things. We hope that the problem will just go away. It is the same reason that some people resist going to the doctor, because if we go the doctor will surely find something wrong that needs fixing. Individuals with drug and alcohol problems perceive that they have the matter under control and that they could quit tomorrow if they wanted. Denial is a powerful force. Even when presented with the evidence, organized religion is at present stuck. It will take both gentle persuaders and confrontational prophets to be able to move the church out of its denial.

Even if we have yet to identity what the problem is or how to solve it, we are painfully aware that one exists. The widening gap between culture and organized religion, the decline in numbers and resources ("the mainline decline") are symptoms of a problem. Other symptoms are the chronic anxiety about money, the fear of losing long-term members by taking a stance on a concern of social justice, and the multiple hat syndrome. No one wants to serve on the nominating committee because it is difficult to find anyone who would be enthusiastic to serve on a committee without having to twist their arm. The pastor has tried to contemporize worship and implement some creative strategies to promote church growth, but nothing seems to be drawing in the crowds. When a church can no longer dwell in denial, they often move into blaming the pastor for their present woes.

When a congregation realizes that there is a problem, they reach what I call, "a point of crisis." They don't have to agree on what the problem is, only that a problem exists. Congregations tend to put more energy into trying to figure out who is causing the problem, than into identifying the root problem underlying the symptoms that are confronting them. For fear that it is the modern worshiper themselves, they point the finger at the pastor and decide to do a congregation-wide evaluation of the pastor's performance to ascertain his or her level of competency, which is often an evaluation based on warm-fuzziness. Other congregations blame the denomination for their stance on social justice issues, such as supporting the right for gay and lesbian persons to be legally married. And still others blame factions that are developing within the local church, which risk splitting the congregation. Internal fighting is a symptom of a larger, systemic problem.

These symptoms indicate that the congregation is experiencing a lack of spiritual energy, that is, the congregation lacks creative energy to transform itself, to heal organizational struggles, and to promote itself as a major player in the cultural environment. I will refer to this lack of spiritual energy as "congregational depression." Depression zaps the energy of an organism and in the process makes an organism turn its attention inward to preserve what energy it has left and to heal its own wounds in order to survive. Depression also causes social isolation. The organism and organization withdraws from previous significant relationships with which it has a history of interaction. It is another symptom of its depression that the church has lost its connection with the culture it managed to have an influential relationship with throughout its history.

My yoga instructor says that we should stretch our bodies, not to the point of excruciating pain, but just to the edge of discomfort. If we push our bodies to the point of pain, we might break a bone or pull a muscle, and then our bodies will naturally stage a rebellion against further movement. Pain signals the body to stop moving before it hurts itself or hurts itself further. A state of shock is the ultimate survival mode for it protects our mind from that which we are unable to grasp at that moment and immobilizes us. Like denial, it protects us from painful feelings. On an emotional level, churches can function in one of three modes: comfort, discomfort, and intense pain. The church that functions in the comfort zone has little willingness to change. The church that functions with intense pain will have little ability to change. So the first step is to move the congregation into the discomfort zone by confronting its denial and equipping it to manage feelings of frustration, hurt, and anger.

When I began talking about the urgency of this matter, I assumed that everyone would be inspired and want to change. But more often the response was to shrug one's shoulders and say, "What do I care? I won't be around in fifty years!" I mistook the state of helplessness as apathy (which has been projected onto the postmodern believer, as mentioned above). The modern worshiper expresses the process of coming out of denial and intense pain this way: "I don't know what it is we need to do to change, so I convinced myself that there wasn't a problem or that the problem was outside of the church."

In its denial, the church has convinced itself that attracting young people will be the magic pill to alleviate its current state of depression. But no postmodern believer is going to be drawn to a depressed organization. In fact, when organisms and organizations become depressed, people tend to stay away because they can feel the intense pain when they walk in the sanctuary, even to a greater extent than those sitting there every week, who perhaps have become numb and desensitized to it. Thus, the most effective way to attract the postmodern generation is to focus on healing congregational depression. The reverse is also observed: we are naturally attracted to healthy people and organizations.

It stands to reason that if a congregation is depressed, and the diagnosis of depression is a lack or suppression of energy, the choice of intervention is to increase its level of spiritual energy. Attracting and assimilating the postmodern believer into the life of the congregation and empowering the postmodern believer to determine the design of the contemporary congregation will also help alleviate the congregation's depression. A sign the church is moving into a healthier mode of functioning will be the presence of the postmodern believer. But it would be unfair to place the responsibility for health upon the postmodern believer, and therefore I write this book for the modern worshiper. Instead of advising starting a new church with new people who are not bogged down by tradition, my intention is to equip the modern worshiper to decide which traditions to bring with them that will be relevant to contemporary need and to grieve those traditions that we need to let go of in order to move forward.

Many church growth specialists observe that the traditional church is experiencing anxiety, and they see this as the problem to be resolved. Anxiety, however, often masks underlying, deep-seated depression. It often manifests itself as an either-or mentality, which is referred to as "splitting." Pastors are either idealized or devalued. Space is either sacred or secular. People are either saved or damned, saint or sinner. The level of participation in a congregation is depicted as either low or high commitment. People are either in or out of the church. Cultural trends are either positive or negative, to be embraced or resisted. When an organization suffers chronic anxiety that stems from long-term depression, the forces that superimpose divisiveness impede spiritual growth and sustain unhealthy modes of functioning.

Anxiety signals that the organism or organization is experiencing a crisis. Anxiety can serve a healing function, a prelude to the movement forward. When anxiety is not denied or avoided, it alerts us that there is a problem to be solved and as long as we do not guard ourselves against it but go with its flow, anxiety helps to access energy to be able to manage change and the stressors that often accompany change. This energy lifts the veil that keeps depression buried and awakens the senses that tell the body that it cannot remain where it is. It can try to go back to a less stressful time or it can go forward and embrace a new paradigm for functioning, that is, a new design for the congregation willing to move forward.

Contemporary congregations are designed to be healthy social systems where change is an ongoing process, continually evolving as culture evolves. The traditional church was also designed to be healthy, but fell victim to a stagnancy that made it unhealthy. Modernity did not corrupt the church; *holding onto* traditions that gradually become incongruent with culture as it shifted from modern to postmodern is what suppressed the congregation's energy and caused its depression. "Contemporary" does not refer to our particular culture; rather, it refers to whatever culture is in vogue at any particular point in history. The concept of contemporary transcends generational fads and culture-specific trends but focuses on the interrelatedness of culture and organized religion.

The postmodern generation will only be attracted to the contemporary congregation if it is receptive to change to access energy and to grow spiritually. I suggest that we view personal spirituality and congregational vitality as two sides of the same coin. The task before us is to design healthy contemporary congregations. I will advocate that this is achieved by the following means:

1. by blending traditional with contemporary trends;

2. by producing what I call "karmic balance," as defined by Jesus, "the measure you give will be the measure you get" (in practice, the energy parishioners put into congregational functioning will be the measure they receive in spiritual energy);

3. by allowing culture to influence organized religion in order to strengthen the connection between the two and to make culture receptive to the influence of organized religion and organized religion receptive to the influence of culture.

These three objectives lead to the goal of spiritual transformation. Organized religion is thus unique from all other social organizations. The uniqueness of spiritual transformation is what will attract the postmodern generation to the church.

OPTIONS AT THE POINT OF CRISIS

In the history of world religions, when a religious organization becomes disconnected from its cultural environment, it has four options to resolve this point of crisis. The crisis is a healthy sign because it demonstrates that the congregation is moving, either beyond their comfort zone or out of their depression. Another sign of health is when religious leaders emerge from within the organization to reform it. Church growth specialists debate whether reformers should be internal movers or external shakers. My task is to transform modern worshipers into internal movers within the congregation.

The first option is to become ultraliberal. The relationship with the umbrella organization, such as the denomination, may be in name only. Cultural change takes priority over institutional change. The objective is to discard anything traditional and replace it with contemporary practice. Everyone connected with the movement chants, "Out with the old and in with the new." The thread that connects the organization with its historical roots is shredded in favor of functioning within the current of cultural trends, which are viewed as positive forces.

The second approach is a liberal one. This approach seeks to interact with culture through the lens of the basic, foundational principles of the religious organization and its theology. This second path allows for diversity beyond the core beliefs, that is, the incarnation of God in Jesus Christ. The church broadly agrees upon the line between what is open to change and what is etched in stone. Spiritual practices shift frequently and experimentation is encouraged. The organization interacts with culture, to influence culture and to be influenced by it, but there are also guiding principles—scripture, through which these cultural trends are assessed and identified as either positive or negative forces. The goal of changing the system is to achieve an optimum balance between traditional and contemporary.

The third approach is conservatism. The perception is that change is warranted within the religious organization because it has been too negatively effected by cultural change. Culture itself, rather than the way the organization functions, needs to be changed. The objective is to "get back on track" and purge the organization of cultural influence by recounting the original design and its guidelines. Here the focus may reach back to the way that the early church functioned as its model for change. It looks backwards in order to inform the adherents how to move forward.

The fourth path is the ultraconservative, often referred to as "extremist." Like the third approach, the perception is that culture is corrupt (often in the form of moral bankruptcy), has contaminated the individual, and is therefore the enemy to be fought against. The objective is to practice a purist form of the religion. If this cannot be achieved within the cultural environment, the church separates itself as a tactic of last resort. Its members may take traditional aspects of the religion with them, but they tend to skew tradition into something more formatted and unchangeable.

Interestingly, all four approaches of reformation intersect at the nexus of culture and religion. Religious organizations exist within cultures (local, national, and global) of social systems that are significantly affected by shifts in cultural trends and significantly affect the direction of culture, especially in the area of social justice. To design contemporary congregations in mainline liberal Protestantism, I will show that the second option will most closely honor our traditions and history while also launching us forward into constructing the next chapter in church history—which I hope will be one that will alleviate the church's depression and help it to feel a sense of pride in its accomplishments and spiritual joy to be chosen as an instrument for the Holy Spirit.

John B. Cobb Jr. shares this view and observes that what energized the early church was its interaction with culture, and that is what we should seek to reclaim, not the practices of the early church.

> In this view our task as Christians is not to recover an original form of life in the church. That form was a creative response to the circumstances of the time. It was shaped out of its past in sensitive interaction with the particularities of its environment.
>
> Our task, as we try faithfully to continue the Christian tradition, is to respond as effectively and appropriately today to

the particularities of our situation as the early church responded in its time.[3]

OVERVIEW OF THIS BOOK

Initially, we voted to offer a second worship service, a "contemporary worship service" and for about two years, it appeared to work quite effectively, but slowly the postmodern believer either began attending the traditional worship service or stopped attending all together. We realized that implementing a second service is not only a form of segregated worship, but it "tokenizes" our efforts to become a contemporary congregation. The premise of this book is that all aspects of congregational functioning need to be "contemporized," that is, influenced by cultural trends. Offering an olive branch to the postmodern believer by contemporizing worship denies the significance of the way the other aspects of congregational functioning also contribute to our spirituality. For the church to reinvent itself, to experience congregational transformation, it must also make significant systemic change in its overall functioning.[4]

Beginning this book with a chapter on contemporary worship may seem in reverse order by the time the reader reaches the end of the book. Out of respect for its traditional seat of honor, I will address the subject of worship in the first chapter. Contemporary worship is a transition between celebrating what the congregation has accomplished through its missionary and social justice activities and praising God for using congregants as the instruments of those activities, and re-energizing those same congregants to go back into the world to engage in ministry again. Without the opportunity to celebrate the ways that God has worked through the servants, to affirm their gifts and talents and to witness to the presence and power of divine intervention, then we are only do-gooders and do not need organized religion. Gathering for worship frames the experience of coming into the church and going out with its cyclical movement that has no beginning and no end.

In chapter 2, I address the relational aspects of organized religion, which are often viewed as a sideline of congregational functioning. For instance fellowship hour is a place to have something to eat and to drink coffee, and some may leave immediately after worship because "church is over." I emphasize the importance of these relationships and define them as "holy interactions." Genuine, open, and affirming relationships are important today more than ever, given the changes in the constitution of the American family. As cultural relational patterns become often characterized by dehumanization, isolation, and competition, organized religion functions to counterbalance those destructive forces. Holy interactions equip the disciples of Christ to go out into the world and engage in evangelism, the subject of chapter 3.

Chapter 4 equips the disciples of Jesus for ministry and chapter 5 examines the avenues for social justice. Because most postmodern believers contact the church for rituals, such as weddings, baptisms, and funerals, I discuss in chapter 6 programs that may be used around these rituals for spiritual transformation. Denominationalism or the unifying umbrella organization of the contemporary congregation is explored in chapter 7.

As a Christian, I take the stance that organized religion can survive but needs to be transformed. We cannot sit back with a wait-and-see attitude about what this change will look like. Nor can we expect that the heavens will open and divine intervention will save the day and return us to the glory days. I believe that God can only work through us, and therefore it will take a concerted effort by dedicated and risk-taking faith communities. We cannot continue to do things the same old way and expect to get different results. Denial is not an option. To do nothing means that the church has accepted its fate of critical care and invokes hospice to provide comfort as it gasps in agony to its death. No, we cannot dwell in denial. The emperor has no clothes because they no longer fit. The church, our symbol of Christianity and its presence in its cultural environment, will only survive when we unite our hearts and minds and allow God's vision to be implemented by designing contemporary congregations.

one | worship

Our church's labyrinth is usually set up in our fellowship hall, but on one warm summer night, the worship team thought that it would be cool to make a labyrinth out of configurations of flowerbeds, sidewalks and bushes out on our front lawn. Arriving early to view this artistic masterpiece, I eagerly took off my shoes to begin walking. Along the grass, the lines were delineated with cornmeal, but where the grass and sidewalk intersected, crude arrows were drawn to show the pilgrim where the lines on the grass resumed. I soon realized I was not in the place I was suppose to be. There were no more arrows pointing me in "the right" direction. Frustrated and annoyed, I kept turning myself around, hoping that inadvertently I would find myself between the lines—but to no avail. So I fell to my knees looked up to the sky and prayed that God would give me the guidance I need to lead the congregation beyond the lines when the arrows are nowhere in sight.

Beyond the lines: we first attempted to contemporize the traditional worship service by introducing contemporary styles of music. But the loud beating music bouncing off the sanctuary walls made some people angry. On one occasion, as the worship team was recessing down the aisle to do the benediction, one man in the last row yelled, "This is barroom music!" (I didn't ask him how he knew this.)

Our intention was not to offend the modern worshiper nor devalue their musical preferences, but to encourage them to be part of the process, and so we shifted gears and instituted a second service that would be a forum for our contemporary music and hopefully keep everyone happy who enjoyed the traditional music.

But an interesting dynamic unfolded. Those who attended the contemporary worship service became curious about the traditional worship service and those with children began attending the traditional worship service because that was the time that Christian education was offered. But the people also flowed in the opposite direction. Those who attended the traditional worship service became curious about the contemporary worship service. They liked the format. Some even liked the music. They would return to the traditional worship service and witness to other modern worshipers, "Have you gone to the contemporary worship service yet? It's wonderful!" And then more modern worshipers would come. The modern worshiper began to function as an evangelist. Eventually, we realized that the modern worshiper and the postmodern believer could worship together in one worship service. They have similar spiritual needs: both are looking for practices that help them to feel spiritually connected to the divine.

What we learned was that the modern worshiper and the postmodern believer respond positively to contemporary and traditional styles of worship. Yet, there are different levels of positive response on the continuum from "really enjoy" to "not my cup of tea." We emphasize two aspects of intergenerational worship (as one aspect of multicultural worship). One, worship is an interaction among worship leaders and worshipers and among the worshipers themselves. It matters who is sitting in the pews on any given Sunday morning. A worship service without a range of ages (as well as other cultural groupings) is segregated worship. Intergenerational worship seeks to provide a variety of worship styles within the same worship experience. Such worship also opens the hearts and minds of worshipers and piques their curiosity to try new and creative ways of worshiping that they might have not tried if all the worshipers were about the same age. Two, worship is not supposed to meet the individual's spiritual needs 100 percent of the time. If the worship team is meeting individual spiritual needs all of the time, then they may be catering to one specific age group. This is the very reason why we do not have a separate contemporary worship service, such as a service specifically geared toward the postmodern generation, because that would teach them that the goal of worship is to fully cater to the individual's spiritual needs.

What does our current worship look like? When we returned to one worship service, we gradually, patiently, and respectfully introduced features of contemporary worship (there were still some holdouts clinging to the traditional format and style). Our worship includes a variety of music, from traditional hymns to praise music to an alternative punk by a band made up of teenagers. Our initial approach was to add rather than subtract, which assured some of our more traditional modern worshipers that aspects of worship that were spiritual to them would not be taken away. We also added liturgical dance, scriptural drama, spiritual meditation, passing of the peace, visual technology, personal witnessing, candle lighting, Bible study (within the worship service!), and a second sermon by one of the pastors other than the senior pastor. And, yes, the worship service exceeds the traditionally designated hour.

Our worship team refers to the movement of the worship service as "the Sesame Street model." Each form of worship—for example, prayer, drama, meditation, music—lasts approximately three minutes, with the only exception being the sermons, which are no longer than ten minutes. We find that the movement of worship and the transitions from one form to the next generate energy and interest ("I wonder what is next?!") and keep everyone's attention focused. Those worshiping with us to see what we are doing often comment, "The worship team holds everyone's attention; how do they do that?" When asked about the length of time for worship, many parishioners respond, "It moves, so you don't notice the time."

For the contemporary congregation, worship is about generating spiritual energy, for example, strength to handle life's challenges and heal traumas of the past to be accessed in our relationships with people outside of the church—personal, professional and peripheral—to work for social justice, which we define as transforming our cultural environment to be more in line with the gospel. Worship is not only about changing who we are to be better able to manage that which threatens to undo us, but we also seek to encourage our community to change for the better, both on the individual and societal level. Spiritual transformation is a process whereby our connection with Jesus is strengthened through his teachings and the way in which he lived his life, and then we pray that God will help us to take what we have learned and apply it to our relationships in other settings.

Our operating principle states: *What you put into worship is what you take with you and what you take with you will be accessible when you need it.* For too long, worshipers felt they put energy into worship that never came back to them, and when the congregation became depressed, there was no energy circulating in worship. In the contemporary church, the optimum balance is to generate and access energy equally throughout each of the modes of functioning. We refer to this as "karmic balance." It means what you put into something is what you get out of it. Jesus says, "The measure you give will be the measure you receive" (Matt. 7:2).

We design contemporary worship to be a celebration of what happens when we return the following week. Because we feel we generate this energy through our interaction among worshipers and access it to have the confidence, the courage, and the strength to be able to go out into the community and engage in social justice, we return to our home base, the sanctuary, our spiritual home, to celebrate that God worked through us to make these changes in the community and to influence our cultural environment. After we celebrate by praising Jesus and thanking God for the gifts that equip us to be disciples, we then pray for refueling. The worship service is geared to acknowledge divine affirmation for the defining moments when we accessed this energy, either as individuals to deal with a difficult situation or as a community to promote social justice.

In this chapter, I address five aspects of contemporary worship. First I say something about our worship team. The second aspect addresses the issue of resistance to change. The third outlines the process of contemporizing the traditional worship service and the fourth examines the delivery of the message in a contemporary format. Rick Warren says, "The message must never change, but the methods (to deliver the message) must change with each new generation."[1] The fifth aspect explores how contemporary worship can function to produce optimal karmic balance.

THE WORSHIP TEAM

At the moment, our worship team consists of myself as the senior pastor (I refer to myself as a "liturgical artist") and two associate pastors who are both African American men (both are seminary trained and ordained in other denominations) and a minister of music. Several lay people also serve as worship leaders, but they change every week. Our worship team is emotionally connected to each other, not only during worship, but we also spend time together at cookouts, musical events, and family celebrations. We like each other and perceive that that "good feeling" comes across in the way we lead worship. We are also people of faith. We believe in our message and, if we do not believe a traditional interpretation of scripture, we have the freedom to talk about what we really believe and how we arrived at that answer.

Traditionally, clergy have been taught that they are the ones who are supposed to lead worship by determining its direction, planning its theme, and being well prepared to deliver a thoughtful sermon on Sunday morning. This not only feeds into the traditional mode of performance and causes much burnout among pastors who do not get much back in return, but when the worship leader overfunctions, that only leaves the congregation the option to underfunction. If worshipers are not encouraged to participate in worship, then the scales tip toward the leaders, not only because of their academic authority but often because "that's why we pay you," causing pastors to feel weighed down to be "on" Sunday morning. When the leaders "hoard'" this spiritual energy, the worshipers will feel they came to watch, not to access spiritual energy.

Worship services should be well planned, with written scripts. We say we are "spirit-driven rather than bulletin-driven," but those who do not depend on the spirit to drive them into preparation before Sunday morning may be depending too much on the spirit and not enough on their own God-given intellect. My brother-in-law said after a worship service recently, "If the pastor said that God love me one more time . . . enough already. . . . I know that God loves me; what else do you have to teach me?" In an academically sophisticated atmosphere characteristic of contemporary culture, the worship service should deliver well-thought-out messages that could not be delivered by lay people. One of the reasons why I feel so passionate that clergy should be fluent in Hebrew and Greek (at least two years of course work in both) is because, I believe this will one of the significant differences between ordained and lay ministers in the contemporary congregation.

The worship team articulates the need for change. Even hearing the word "change" will make some modern worshipers cringe and cling to their beloved traditions. In a traditional congregation, the worship team, including the senior pastor, will need to address the dynamics of resistance. If the senior pastor is resistant to the change and will not function as a mover of the movement, efforts by others on the team may be sabotaged. The worship leaders should expect resistance. If there were no resistance to change, the church would be dead. The very act of resistance can be a way to access energy that congregational depression has suppressed. Resistance is a neglected aspect of church growth because most specialists today suggest a church-within-a-church model or church planting. Both represent new churches that are not steeped in tradition that is ingrained in its functioning. But resistance to change is a natural part of the process of transforming the traditional church that must be dealt with by the worship team.

REDIRECTING THE ENERGY OF RESISTANCE

Signs of resistance mean that the organization has energy to be accessed and is willing and able to move beyond its depressed condition. Negative reactions to change may be expressed by the following concerns. "Don't young people want to worship the same way we worship, and if not, what's wrong with the way we do it?" "Suppose we make all these changes and then young people don't come? Can we then go back to the way we have always done it?" "Aren't we just buying into the philosophy of the megachurches, who just want to increase their numbers?" "Why do we need more people when we can't meet all the spiritual needs of the ones we have now?" "My family has supported this church for generations. Why should we cater to those who have never set foot in here?" And my personal favorite, "Worship is suppose to be boring; why change it?"

When the traditional style of worship was implemented fifty years ago, it *was* contemporary to the modern worshiper. But time passed. The cultural environment changed. The beloved pastor resigned. Amidst all these changes, the worship service became a stable, predictable arrow pointing to God. *Because* culture changed so rapidly and dramatically over the last fifty years, the modern worshiper invested in that which they could control, namely, maintaining the worship format with its traditional forms. The system itself, as a collection of individuals experiencing the change of culture, functioned to counterbalance cultural change (known as "homeostatic balance") and produce a stabilizing force. Keeping worship a constant, using the same format and styles from week to week, year to year, may actually have helped the modern worshiper manage these cultural changes and allow culture to benefit. Organized religion may have been the stabilizing force that allowed culture to change.

When we began talking about "change," we emphasized three things. First, we emphasized the *urgency* of this situation and confronted the delusion that the postmodern generation would one Sunday morning wake up and in one sweeping movement see the light and begin attending a traditional worship service. We had to agree that it was not going to happen that way. We spoke often of this day and age as a "window of opportunity" to appeal to the next generation of worshipers who would embrace our mission to keep the traditional church alive and well.

Second, we stressed that the modern worshiper would benefit from these changes. If it matters who is in worship, then attracting the postmodern generation would generate new energy in the service itself. We selected an initial target group for our evangelism: the adult children of our modern worshipers. The congregants had complained for years, "I raised them in the church. I don't understand why they don't come and bring their children." So we focused on these concerns of the modern worshiper. They were more willing to engage in such a pilgrimage if their own children and grandchildren would benefit. Because the postmodern believer tends to attract other postmodern believers, this proved to be an effective strategy to get the first few postmodern believers to be willing to worship in a traditional context. One of the biggest obstacles to overcome initially is that when a postmodern believer comes to worship and sees that mostly modern worshipers and no one their own age, there is a low probability that they will return. So this strategy helped us to overcome this potential obstacle.

Third and most importantly, we stress this movement as God's vision for our church. Those who are the movers of contemporizing our worship genuinely believe that God is calling us to make these changes, to articulate this vision, and to call to the congregation on a consistent basis in the worship service itself. We did not call a congregational meeting to vote on whether or not to move toward becoming a contemporary congregation. The pilgrimage to attract the postmodern believer was a pilgrimage of faith. If we truly believe that when we worship together, God bestows blessings on us through the worship experience and through our holy interactions with one another, then why wouldn't we want our adult children and grandchildren to also share in those blessings?

EVALUATING THE STYLES OF TRADITIONAL WORSHIP

Once the modern worshiper was willing (some more than others) to participate in this movement, we took on the process of evaluating which forms of worship were producing spiritual energy and which ways had become outdated in the sense that they no longer met anyone's spiritual needs. This process involves trust and honesty among those engaging in the task of evaluation (holy interactions), for fear that someone might say, "How could you not like that?" and might accuse another of not being a faithful Christian. We asked questions like, "Does that kind of prayer help you feel closer to God?" We also asked questions related to our design for contemporizing aspects of the traditional worship service, such as, "Do you think that the prayer would be enhanced if we also had music accompanying it?" Not everyone was asked every question. We also expected that there would be some initial resistance to the changes, simply because they were changes, but this process gave the worship team some freedom and creativity to experiment with changes in worship.

While the worship service will change, not *everything* will change. The approach we took was to blend contemporary with traditional. We examined each aspect of the worship service to discern whether it fell into one of three categories: 1) it makes us feel closer to God, 2) it may make someone else feel closer to God, and 3) it most likely doesn't make anyone feel closer to God. Responsive readings that used old English went into the third basket. This is not to say that understanding the language was a criterion, since many modern worshipers like hearing the Bible read in Hebrew and Greek. Calls to worship and the assurance of pardon were considered out of date, the call to worship because of its responsive nature and the assurance of pardon because we decided not to "make people feel bad about themselves in the first five minutes of worship." We did not initially subtract any of the forms of worship until the momentum for change was moving forward.

When a form of worship was put into the elusive third category, there were four options for its next life. The first was that we could figuratively put it to sleep with the intention that it might be reawakened at another time when it was more aligned with a changed culture. The second was that we could continue to use it in worship with the hope that the energy of a different group of worshipers might give that form new life. In the third option, we could "tweak" the traditional form into something more contemporary. The way in which we pray has been tweaked to include music, sometimes with the congregation standing, other times facing a direction, sometimes with hands stretched toward heaven. Sometimes, we tweak a traditional hymn by giving it some bounce with drums and a guitar. The fourth option was that we could juxtapose a traditional and contemporary style of the same form of worship side by side. An example of this is that our opening music (after the first sermon) often begins with a lively, hand-clapping praise song and goes right into a traditional hymn.

Initially, most forms of worship made it into category one, but gradually some were placed in category three. When the modern worshiper began paying closer attention to whether or not various forms of worship produce spiritual energy (and the worship team speaks about what spiritual energy is and how to experience it), they began to admit that there were many worship styles that had been embraced because they had been practiced for so many years but had really lost their collective meaning. "Why *do* we do that?" Any change that was made was not etched in stone, and so we had some freedom to experiment with new forms. We found that most resistance to a new form expressed a fear that it would become permanent and not subject to feedback (because that had been the traditional way of implementing change). Our approach empowered the modern worshiper to worship outside of their comfort zone without a cherubim placed in front of their garden as a point of no return. If congregational anxiety increased to an unmanageable degree, we simply brought back a more familiar form of worship.

Some forms of worship were still working but needed to be tweaked. Most of us like to sing songs from our hymnal (we use the *Celebration Hymnal*), but we also enjoy learning songs by repeating the soloist. We do not use visual technology for singing the hymns because we feel that presents the same issue as the hymnal itself, that is, the focus is on reading the lyrics rather than making eye contact with others and thus generating energy. Prayers are not always practiced by bowing our head, closing our eyes or looking down at our feet. They are image-based (invite the participant to "image" or create an image in their mind of the subject of the prayer) and they are sometimes said standing up with hands held up to heaven or facing a specific direction, such as east, especially if praying for a specific group of people, such as the soldiers in Iraq.

The offertory was the most debated form of worship. The idea proposed was to collect the money on the way out or to leave a basket in the back of the sanctuary. The postmodern believer often complains that the church is only looking for money to sustain itself. Some modern worshipers stamped their feet, complaining that the postmodern believer needs to learn early on that they too are responsible for the financial responsibilities of the church. Others view stewardship as another path toward generating spiritual energy and feeling close to God, and so they think the offertory should remain in its traditional form within the worship format itself. That discussion continues to this day.

CONTEMPORARY DELIVERY OF THE THEOLOGICAL "ANSWER"

Prior to the advent of television, (and it's difficult for the postmodern believer to even imagine that there was such a time), there was radio. Many modern worshipers fondly remember listening to the old-time classics. By spending time just listening, the modern worshiper developed a very sophisticated intellectual skill: they can hear a story and attach pictures to that story in their imagination. Because that was the only way to follow the story, the modern worshiper imprinted images that can be accessed during the listening process. So when the modern worshiper comes to church and listens to a sermon, they are quite adept at picturing what the preacher is talking about. For instance, if the sermon is about Jesus walking on the water encouraging Peter to do likewise as an act of faith, they can imagine the scene. Being able to image the sermon is one of the most effective ways of making it relevant and taking it with you so that it comes to mind on Monday morning or when a situation arises that requires that spiritual wisdom and guidance.

The postmodern believer has not developed such a capacity. To them, audio without visuals means their technological device is broken and needs to be fixed. Having been raised with TV and video games, the postmodern believer needs the visual to engage in many activities. The audio can even be turned down or off, and the game can still be played. Auditory sounds are usually in the form of music that helps drive the action and therefore are noted as background enhancers to the visual pictures. Audio is also a portable background, with iPod devices used for exercise, riding on the bus, studying, and so on. For the postmodern believer, music is often in the background and so we use musical accompaniment through most of the prayers, spiritual meditation, and other parts of worship that traditionally had none.

The contemporary congregation uses audio and visual means rather than relying solely on sound to generate spiritual energy.

Whereas the modern worship uses audio primarily and visuals secondarily, the postmodern believer responds primarily to visuals and secondarily to audio stimulus. This is an important point to stress. The problem is that the modern worshiper does not want "a large screen descending from our beautiful chancel!" But there are other ways of creating visual images. Contemporary preaching takes an image and builds the sermon around that image. Art work displayed around the sanctuary or on the chancel can be quite effective if it reflects this imagery theme. Video devices that can be projected or power point presentations with a portable screen that can be brought in and taken out after the sermon may be another option.

One of the major differences between traditional and contemporary preaching is that the modern worshiper responds to the traditional authority of the preacher giving the worshiper *the* answer. The postmodern believer wants to know how the preacher arrived at that specific answer. They are more interested in the process of arriving at answers than the content of the preacher's answer. They ask, "How do you know that?" or "Why do you believe that?" This should not be viewed as disrespectful or a challenge to the preacher's authority, but a request to be empowered for their own spiritual quest for answers. Contemporary culture, especially in our academic institutions, asks those kinds of questions in order to establish reliability. When one can re-create the process and find one's own content (answer), then the process itself has validity.

In contemporary worship, there is an expectation that the preacher will share a personal illustration of divine intervention. This requires some insight and skill, because in a healthy congregation, the pastor walks a fine line between what is appropriate to share and what is not appropriate and crosses professional boundaries. Throughout my ministry, I have functioned with the guiding rule not to share stories that belong to my children, because they should be able to live their lives and not worry that an incident may end up as a sermon illustration on Sunday morning. By the grace of God, I have had enough stuff happen to me personally to fill twenty-five years of sermon illustrations.

Traditionally, sources of authority are hierarchically arranged, but throughout the history of Christianity, the placement of these sources has been rearranged. Protestants defend the sole authority of scripture as the Word of God, and when religious questions are asked, we turn to the Bible as the book of answers. Personal religious experience, even when that experience is reflected in the experience of biblical characters, has not been held with the same degree of authority and conviction. When our personal religious experience contradicts the Bible, as when the laws of the Bible are culturally based, we can either allow these two sources of authority to continue to be in competition for status, or we can attempt to reconcile them by challenging the English interpretation. An example of this tension is whether or not the Bible has anything to say about the subject of homosexuality.

In contemporary congregations, multiple answers are tolerated. This is not to suggest that contemporary congregations will "water down" the religion of Christianity nor the tenets of the Protestant faith, only that we acknowledge that within one congregation, within any faith community, we are privately not going to all agree on the answer to every theological question. We are also aware that specific cultural groupings often derive their own answers based on their ethnic experience or cultural heritage. Those who have experienced oppression, for instance, may answer the question about the ways we witness to God's intervention in the world in terms of liberation from the power structures.

Traditional preaching assumed that there was one right answer, and the preacher knew what the one right answer was, often based on the right answer as determined by our church fathers long ago. Because our church fathers and translators of the Bible into English were part of the dominant group, the translation into English often reflects their cultural perspective. Thus, the historical pattern of arriving at answers has been that those in positions of dominance are the ones who decide the right answer for those who are marginalized. A similar process is at work if we encourage the modern worshiper to be the only ones who contemporize the congregation without inviting the postmodern believer to be part of the process and to work together. The "old" idea of missionary activity was that the missionaries held the right answer for those who needed their help.

Answers also change over time. Nowhere do we witness to this more than in scientific inquiry. What we thought about the universe and the human body has changed radically in the last fifty years. As with science, willingness to continually test-drive certain theories is the way that the postmodern believer will approach organized religion. The answer that made sense to their parents and grandparents may not be the same answer that works for them, only because culture has changed and theological answers have to make sense within our own cultural environment. Answers are subject to revision based on scientific advances, archeological discoveries, and more. In mainline liberal Protestantism, when a change is made in one of these cultural areas, our answer may change in order to be congruent, or at least more aligned, with this new knowledge. An example of this may be whether or not individuals who are dying have the right to take their own life if the quality of that life is one of suffering.

If contemporary congregations function by tolerating multiple answers, what is the glue that unites a faith community? The answer may be location, but I think it too simplistic an answer. It may also be cultural grouping, especially for immigrants coming into this country and desiring to pass their cultural traditions and religious practices on to their children as a way to preserve the connection with their ethnic background. Not much has been researched on how much economic circumstance or class may also have a significant impact on uniting a community of faith. The traditional answer to this question for Christians has been a belief in Christ's resurrection. We believe that that traditional answer is our core belief. Core beliefs do not change, only what we call "peripheral beliefs" that surround that core belief.

Does this mean that a contemporary faith community has to tolerate "crazy" answers? Not at all. Individual answers still have to respect sources of authority: personal religious experience and scripture. When someone approaches me, as a liturgical artist proficient in Hebrew, and professes "but it's in the Bible!" I ask them to show me where. They then usually turn the page to a stock answer that they have been fed to them by a religious authority figure. I open my Hebrew Bible and point out that the one word they have based their entire argument upon is an inaccurate translation. The verb *shakab*, "to lie beside," in Leviticus 18:22 is an example. This verse is often used to denounce homosexuality. The Bible speaks about sex often and there is a common verb for it, so if the writer intended to speak about sex, he would have used a different verb. Meanwhile, we have a whole generation of preachers who are convinced that they are preaching the "right" answer but who do not read Hebrew and/or Greek.

The pastor is held up on a pedestal as a model of ethical conduct for every parishioner to emulate. When the pastor falls from this projection, the modern worshiper either denies that the incident happened and rushes to the pastor's defense or feels that their faith has been

"dashed" by this betrayal and may abandon their faith in the organization. (Many modern worshipers do not differentiate their faith in the
organization from their personal faith in God.) They come to church
to hear that answer and to project power and idealization onto the
preacher as the source of authority for all theological answers.

The postmodern believer also views preaching as ethical instruc-
tion but responds, ""I don't need to go to church. I'm already a good
person." Organized religion appears to be a place where people do
what they do because they have been told to do it from a parental figure. In the postmodern believer's eyes, this approach infantilizes the
believer ("Do they need someone else to tell them what to do?"). Given
the recent revelation of sexual abuse by clergy, the postmodern believer
sees the modern worshiper's placing the preacher on a pedestal as po-
tentially contradictory, as taking advice from someone who "does not
preach what he professes." The postmodern believer says, "Why
would I listen to what they say when they did what they did?" In the
contemporary congregation, the preacher will be seen less as a model
of ethical conduct and more as what is often referred to as "authentic,"
that is, "a real person" with their own limitations and struggles.

PRODUCING KARMIC BALANCE

When I am doing yoga, it matters little who is sitting next to me. In
fact, the goal of this form of meditation is to tune out any of the other
people in the room. Not so in organized religion. It matters who is
sitting next to me in the pew because worship is an interaction between leader and worshipers and among worshipers. I am aware of
the person sitting next to me in the pew; that person's presence actually enhances my experience of worship. The constitution of the
worshipers in a congregation on any given Sunday sets the tone of
worship and the way in which the worshipers respond to that tone,
to its movement and vitality. It also invokes the dance of the spirit,
but the spirit dances to different tunes. When worshipers invest energy in worship, it multiplies and vibrates and creates a collective
connection to the divine Spirit.

Eastern religions function on the principle of karma, which in its
Western definition translates as *what you put into something (in terms of
deeds and energy) comes back to you* in equal balance. My yoga instructor will say encouragingly, "come on, everyone, we only get out of it
what we put into it." In a consumer-driven society it also means "you

get what you pay for." The same can be said for our interaction during the worship service. What we put into the worship service, as worshipers, is what comes back to us. If we come to worship enthusiastically looking forward to what God may do, we will generate energy and be more receptive to experiencing that energy. But if we put little energy into it, we will receive little in return. In depressed congregations, karmic imbalance is often the "problem." If parishioners participate in congregational functioning, whether as religious leaders or helping out with the bake sale, and do not feel appreciated, valued, and affirmed for their contribution, they will eventually burn out. When this happens in a congregation, there is little energy floating in its mist, and people will not want to get involved. Then when others are complaining and criticizing, energy is zapped from every direction.

How do we generate spiritual energy in a worship service? Traditionally, the sole pastor functions to produce energy in the worship service and the worshipers come to watch this process. But the more the pastor functions, the less energy is available to those who have come to watch the performance. The contemporary trend is toward empowering worship participants to participate in worship. While preaching the message may continue to be the domain of the ordained pastor who knows the biblical languages, most of the rest of the worship service can be done by someone else. When the pastor is exhausted and feels drained after worship, it indicates that the pastor is overfunctioning. If so, it follows that the congregation is underfunctioning. This is how congregations become depressed.

Pastors have been trained to overfunction, and overfunctioning tends to meet their own personal needs. Being a pastor of a church comes with an incredible amount of projected power, prestige, and status (at least within the organization). When a person does not feel power in other relationships, being a religious leader may be the quickest way of experiencing power. Because we do not educate pastors about how to handle this power and how it is related to spiritual energy, that power is often misused and, too often, abused.

Parishioners project this power and place clergy on a pedestal. This intrapsychic process may be a source of self-esteem for the pastor. Key, then, to designing a contemporary worship service is to find ways to affirm the pastor's functioning as the pastor who equips the disciples of Jesus to experience spiritual energy in worship so that they can go out and do the ministry that needs to be done.

Thus we provide opportunities for worshipers to be involved in worship, either as leaders in the worship team or as participants in worship. Many access energy by sharing their love of music, either by singing or playing an instrument. Others share their artwork, and in a neutral colored space such as a typical sanctuary, this artwork can stand out visually. We say that there is something for everyone to do. A scriptural drama team dramatizes the scripture. Rather than having one person read the scripture and the others listen to it, or as stated above, try to listen to the words and picture the situation, scriptural drama helps people to imagine the situation and, perhaps more importantly, imagine themselves in that situation, which then equips them to better deal with the situation. Sometimes this is rehearsed and well planned out, and at other times it is ad hoc, which can be really funny when something happens spontaneously or when someone rescues themselves from a mistake. It reflects everyday life, which itself is unscripted.

We also reserve a time in the worship service for witnessing. Individuals share a personal story through which they witnessed divine intervention and then speak of the transformational nature of that intervention. "This is how I was changed because of this experience." In congregations that are used to functioning in a traditional mode, witnessing can be a leap of faith. We have found there are two ways of doing this. One is to open the microphone to anyone who would like to come forward and share a story. Another is for the worship team to select one worshiper before the worship service (so they can write down their story and read it if they so desire, which encourages people who would not otherwise feel comfortable witnessing to do so). We have done it both ways, but we find that the second way reduces the incidence of "rambling."

A second way to generate spiritual energy in the worship service is through an equal balance of stillness and movement. There is an old joke among clergy that we look out into the congregation and see what is affectionately referred to as "the oil painting effect." No one moves, no one smiles, and no one laughs. Contemporary worship is often distinguished from traditional as more "lively." We allow moments for getting up and moving around as well as moments to be still. Movement allows us to speak to God and stillness gives us the opportunity to listen for a response, and so both are avenues for accessing spiritual energy.

Liturgical dance is another effective way to produce movement in the worship service. Whereas preaching the word tends to be associated with our thinking function, liturgical dance touches us on an emotional level. It communicates feeling and witnesses to the movement of the Spirit. It is also wonderful to see the children and teenagers feel so passionately about their participation in the worship service. In the immediate aftermath of September 11, 2001, the liturgical dance troupe choreographed a dance to the "Ave Maria" and held candles as they danced. It moved many in the congregation to tears. Those who had previous reservations about liturgical dance—that it was sacrilegious, as in "kids dancing in the aisles!"—now embrace this form of worship wholeheartedly.

Perhaps the most controversial issue with respect to movement has been whether or not the congregation should be clapping. Some see it as a way to move and expend energy in the worship experience; others view it as a residue of seeing worship as a performance. Some perceive that the senior pastor should "do something" but others realize that the senior pastor doesn't have that kind of control over the congregation. I suspect that it is something to complain about in the midst of other changes in movement, such as interacting verbally with the religious leaders as they lead worship. What is interesting is that the congregation only used to clap for music and have recently begun clapping for other aspects of worship, such as baptisms. When something is on the increase, it is usually a sign that it is not going away any time soon.

To experience stillness, we use spiritual meditation, which is led by a worship leader and invokes an image or scene through which a spiritual experience is set up, but the emphasis is on the resources of the individual. For instance, a scene may be a guided image and then the worship leader asks, "What do you see?" Each person's answer will be different. The goal is to have an encounter with the Divine in a way that allows resolution to a specific problem or concern. Because worshipers may have different concerns, this sets up a opportunity for each worshiper to find a solution to a problem that works for them. Spiritual meditation is another form through which to arrive at an answer.

Energy-producing worship is transformational in that it shifts the worshipers' perspectives to deal with their personal relationships and to engage in social justice. Worshipers exit the worship experience feeling good about themselves. They feel equipped to handle personal problems as well as motivated to go out into the community and be the presence of Jesus. Our worship service transitions with a commissioning and a blessing. The commissioning sends Jesus' disciples forward for service. A religious leader may instruct worshipers to smile at ten people whom they pass on the street this week or to pray five times a day while facing the church for what is going on in Darfur. We might invite everyone to return that afternoon for a protest rally or to pray instead of getting angry at a coworker or family member. Transitioning from worship to the community means to take the spiritual energy that you have received with you in order to invest it to influence the community in positive ways. Transformation of the worshiper may take place in the context of worship, but it is to be passed along (not kept or hoarded).

In contemporary congregations, attending worship every week is a cyclical process of our functioning. The sanctuary is the sacred place of worship where we come to be energized by the Spirit, to be equipped for service through the blessing of spiritual gifts. Through worship we go out into the community to engage in social justice, and then we bring others back with us. When we return to worship the following week, we come to celebrate this process and to witness not only the spiritual transformation that took place within us through worship, but within our community. When others witness this transformation, they want to come with us to experience the source of that transformation.

two | **fellowship**

I take any opportunity I have to talk with someone outside the church, whether sitting on a park bench waiting for fireworks or waiting to be seated in a restaurant. I strike up a conversation and ask, "Why do you think people go to church?" I am less concerned about why an individual happens to attend a specific church because that is often related to location or to a pastor's personality. If the person seems to be enjoying this particular topic of conversation, my next question is, "What do you think the church has to offer that no other social organization can offer?" My inquiry seeks to discern whether the modern worshiper and the postmodern believer have similar perceptions of what the church has to offer and how far apart those perceptions might be.

The most common response I've received (by far!) among modern worshipers has related to fellowship. "When I had a major crisis in my life, it was the support of my church family that helped me to get through it." The modern worshiper expressed an emotional connection when they spoke about the church they belong to, even if they spoke of other variables, such as the pastor or the pastor's preaching. Many recalled days in the past when the church was "the center" of their lives, not only their place of worship on Sunday mornings. They spoke of being involved in world missions through making kits to send. Or they remembered the times when there were enough young adults to form a cell group within the congregation and how they used to raise funds for missions by putting on a talent show. In almost all of the responses from modern worshipers, there was a noted difference in congregational functioning between the then and now. "It isn't like it used to be." When asked why they continue to attend, they responded, "The people."

When asked "Why do you think that people go to church?" the post-modern believer most often answered, "People go to church to worship God." Their answers had little, if anything, to do with human relationships. When asked a follow-up question, "Do you think the people know each other?" the answer was "No. I imagine people try to get in and out of there as quick as possible." But when asked if the church was the only place to do this, they responded "God is everywhere so the church is not the only place to spend time with God. But people who go to church think they have a monopoly on God." I asked, "Have you ever thought about going to a church?" Most said, "Yes," but there was often a "but" attached to the affirmative. The perception is that the church contains everybody's "grandmother." When asked, "Do you need a grandmother-like person in your life?" They looked sad and answered, "Yes."

I came to realize that one of the church's best assets is hidden from view. For so long we have focused on worship as our "door" to attracting people to our congregation. The traditional church has placed most of its energy into the worship service and not enough into its other modes of functioning. The worship service is viewed as a major force in producing karmic balance, that is, the interaction among worshipers. But it is fellowship—the forming of emotional bonds with each other—that is the interaction that makes worship "work." In a community of faith where no one has an emotional connection with one another, worship would be a different experience than one in which there are opportunities for emotional attachment among worshipers.

In postmodern culture, there are several opportunities for individuals to affiliate with social organizations, from soccer teams to organizations where the purpose is networking, such as Rotary Club. These organizations also meet relational needs. Individuals must pick and choose selectively which social organizations in which to invest their energy based on their expectations of which organizations will yield the most energy in return. Organizations that tend to drain the individual of their energy and not replace that energy in return are organizations to be avoided. When postmodern believers find their way into a congregation, which is so happy to see them because it means an extra pair of hands for the harvest, they may feel overwhelmed by the "welcome." They are likely not to return and likely to seek out another social organization where the karmic energy is more balanced.

Social organizations have to compete with each other for the postmodern believer's attention. The church throws up its hands and says, "Why should we have to compete; we are a church!" But the reality is that if the church takes itself out of the competition, the church will die. How to we compete? We market our strengths, our uniqueness, our specialties, what we do well, and our history of creating emotional and supportive relationships. Our church likes to say "We are an umbrella for when it rains." By investing energy into developing relationships with those in the church, one can access that energy as strength to get through difficult times in life as they unfold. The objective is to turn around the perception that church is "one more thing to do in an already busy week" into the perception that church is the grounding base that energizes us to be involved in everything else we do during the week.

Postmodern culture is also characterized by fewer opportunities for cooperative social interactions, even if there is an increase in social organizations themselves (and thus more, not less, competition). When the individual hooks up with a social organization, the focus is often task-oriented, as we have become a multitasking culture. One can be part of an organization and not know others very well, such as working in a place of big business where corporate expectations of production and alienation overshadow relating to others (as well as to the product). The Internet, e-mail, and cell phones have replaced face-to-face interaction. We do not know our neighbors. Our family members are all over the country. Friends come and go as big businesses downsize and transfer their employees to other parts of the country. For children, almost all of their daily interactions are competitive, whether in the classroom, on the playground, or on the soccer field.

Furthermore, modern worshipers have taught me that relationships with other modern worshipers are "different" from other relationships, such as those with family, friends, neighbors, and colleagues, even if they appear to be "social." In other social organizations there is an expectation of "keeping up appearances." If an individual has a crisis, that crisis is only to be shared in a social organization if it cannot be hidden from others. But in a religious organization, people can be authentically present. They express a comfort level with other modern worshipers that touches the core of their being and makes them feel genuinely connected with each other. "We can be ourselves in the church." These social relationships in organized religion stand out from social relationships in other organizations.

We believe that we form relationships within the church so that the Holy Spirit can work through us to provide comfort, encouragement, insight, strength, and so on to others. Whereas the focus in other social organizations is on the human-to-human connection, we believe that in a church the focus is on the human-to–Holy Spirit connection, but that connection manifests itself through human-to-human interaction. We embrace a relational theology through which being a disciple of Jesus means that we have signed up for service to be an instrument of God's blessing through each other: We believe that God's intervention can only happen through a human agent. An important function of the contemporary congregation, then, is to teach healthy patterns of relating and interacting with others.

It has only been recently that emotional connections and patterns of relating have been examined for their maintenance or relational value versus their task orientation. How many times have I heard leaders break up the conversation in a cell group by saying, "Let's get back to the reason (the task) we are here." Relationships have been traditionally viewed as a means toward an end: One develops relationships with others only to the extent needed to accomplish the task at hand. In the postmodern view, relationships are the threads that weave a community together, and in a contemporary congregation, the process of weaving itself is a witness to the work of the Holy Spirit. We refer to the process of allowing the Holy Spirit to work through us to develop relationships within a congregation as "holy interactions." They are more than conversations; they are the spiritual energy that is passed from one human spirit to another and back again.

Holy interactions are different from social relationships in three ways. First and foremost, what constitutes a healthy relationship is not derived from psychosocial theories, but from the life of Jesus. We model our relationships on the way that Jesus lived his life, interacted with others, and stood up for those who were not in a position to stand up for themselves, for example, the marginalized. The scriptural testimony of how Jesus lived and the emotional connection that he made with others in order to bring peace and reconciliation, sometimes through confrontation and conflict, are the guidelines for our assessment of what a healthy relationship should look like. When we are interacting with others in a way that we believe that Jesus would interact, then we are giving the Holy Spirit a receptacle to do its work.

Second, holy interactions are formed for the purpose of conversing about faith. If the three most avoided topics of conversation are politics, sex, and religion, we intend to provide a trusting place for individuals to talk about their faith and what they really believe without fear that someone else will try to convert them to believe something else or tell them what they believe is "wrong." Because we honor individual's personal religious experience, we respect the process of how they arrived at their answer. We may not agree with their conclusion, but often after we hear their story and feel its emotional content, we can at least understand how they arrived at that specific answer. Our objective is to break down the obstacles that have traditionally obstructed people of faith from talking about that faith and to provide a space for discussion.

Third, in a caring and supporting environment, the church, unlike other social organizations, is in a position to confront dysfunctional patterns of relating that often isolate the individual from experiencing meaningful and intimate relationships with others in other settings of their life. "The church has to love you, but not everyone else does." This doesn't mean that we have to approve of one's behavior, especially if we see that behavior or pattern of relating as counter to the way that Jesus lived his life. Because we put energy into forming relationships, we are thus in a position to be able to say something, to confront the person and to teach them healthier ways of relating. But the difference is that we then encourage that person to go out and "practice" these news ways of relating with others. This transfer of learning extends to family and friends who might not be able to confront the behavior for fear of rejection or anger.

THE FORMATION OF "HEALTHY" HOLY INTERACTIONS

Christianity has long embraced Pauline imagery that its organization is a collection of sisters and brothers united in Christ. This level of intimacy emphasizes that these relationships are not "friendships" but should reflect a stronger emotional and spiritual connection. A symptom of congregational depression is when modern worshipers view their relationships with other modern worshipers as "friendships" that are not any different from any other friendships in any other social organizations. Jesus may have been referring to this emotional connection when he says, "You shall leave your brothers and sisters." The word "leave" here in the Greek does not necessarily mean to leave either physically or emotionally, but to rise above, such as to overcome dysfunctional patterns of relating in one's family of origin.

The foundation of all relationships is trust. The place to begin to form holy interactions is to design a setting in which people can trust one another. When someone feels betrayed, the design should be conducive to allowing the expression of that feeling. What often prevents people from expressing feeling hurt or betrayed is the fear of causing someone else to be hurt or that the hurt could lead to physical violence and/or abandonment. Too often, an individual's feelings are hurt and they are never heard from again. No one in the church reaches out to them because no one feels "qualified" to deal with the injured person's feelings and fears that they will "get an earful." So the congregation practices avoidance, which is not what Jesus would do. Meanwhile, the individual who felt hurt is now hurt seven times seven because no one from their beloved faith community reaches out to them.

At the same time, in a contemporary congregation trust needs to be balanced with safe environmental policies. With the recent disclosure of sexual abuse by clergy, I do not advocate that congregations promote an atmosphere where everyone is to be trusted without guidelines. Even if only one out of a hundred people might take advantage of a trusting relationship, the problem is you cannot tell who that one may be. A contemporary congregation designs a boundary where everyone is a potential betrayer of one's trust. Traditional congregations have excessive bylaws for functioning in terms of who can serve on a committee and for how long, and yet they neglect to publicly declare appropriate patterns of relating.

Individuals learn how to relate to others through their family of origin. These patterns of relating are replayed in all their subsequent relationships, including relationships with pastors and parishioners. When these relationships are unhealthy (and healthy versus unhealthy should be viewed as a continuum rather than an either-or) to the extent that they cause problems, the congregation is responsible to teach healthy patterns of relating. Family members may be unaware that these patterns of relating are dysfunctional because they relate the same way. Colleagues in a business setting may complain to a supervisor. Neighbors may just avoid the person. Such indirectness rarely is effective in helping someone to change their behavior. A Christian community is in the business of forming and nurturing healthy relationships and is therefore in a position to directly confront with compassion the unhealthy pattern of relating and/or to model healthier patterns through interactions with others.

Unfortunately, individuals who manifest unhealthy patterns of relating tend to get squeezed out of the congregation because no one wants to have to deal with them or their problem. They may be difficult to get along with. If their pattern of relating is to be critical of others' contributions to congregational life, there will be a natural tendency to avoid that person and not ask them to participate on major projects. Because in other social settings these people are often pushed away from the core group, they end up feeling lonely and isolated and so may turn to the church as a place of refuge. But the function of a congregation is not to provide another place where everyone enables them to continue to manifest their dysfunctional behavior. It is a place where individuals work at trusting each other in order to tell each other what they would tell no one else: to say something that no one else has the courage to say.

Organized religion seems to be a magnet for attracting individuals with unhealthy patterns of relating. In healthy social organizations, the choice of intervention is "to get rid of them." Most churches follow this practice by simply weeding out those with dysfunctional social skills because they have the "work of Christ" to attend to. Pastors lament, "I have enough on my plate. Now, I am expected to also be a therapist?" In the past, these people were labeled as "clergy killers" and were to be avoided like the plague. If a congregation managed to exorcise them from their midst, then they didn't have to deal with the problem. At the very least, the approach was to navigate around them. When they end up at the church down the street to replay the same dynamics with another pastor and another congregation, the first congregation does not seem to feel they have any accountability for the pain and frustration they enable to be inflicted on the sister congregation.

In a contemporary congregation, it is not the pastor who is responsible for acting as "therapist," but it should entail a united effort between religious leaders (including the pastor) and the congregation. Healthy congregations create and sustain healthy patterns of relating, which produce healthy individuals. On the cable television show *The Dog Whisperer*, the dog trainer interviews an owner whose dog is fighting with other dogs or not able to functionally relate to other dogs. He brings the dysfunctional dog to his own home, where he has trained a functional pack of dogs to get along with each other. A combination of the pack's expectations for appropriate dog behavior and his own leadership produce a dog that relates functionally to other dogs and is then returned to the owner in the community.

Holy interactions need to be healthy patterns of relating because they reflect the way that individuals will experience their connection with God. When the individual feels that "everyone is against me and nobody likes me," he or she will be difficult to convince that "Jesus loves you." The way in which we image God is often based on our parental images. If those parental images conjure up negative feelings, they will need to be replaced with positive experiences of parent-like figures within the church. When parishioners experience the love, caring, compassion, power, support, acceptance, and affirmation from others within their religious community, they will experience those attributes as flowing from the divine source.

HOLY CONVERSATIONS

We are a religious organization that is embarrassed to talk about religion. The unspoken norm is that one's faith is "a private matter." While I realize this may be a regional observation, and I serve Jesus in New England, the practice in many congregations is that the pastor preaches the truth and fills the minds of the parishioners with that truth. The process of indoctrination is unilateral, from one mind to another, rather than as an exchange of experiences. The focus in the traditional church on preaching has influenced this conversational flow: the pastor can speak about their faith but no one else is given an opportunity to do so. The contemporary congregation will provide a forum through which holy conversations are invited, encouraged, and supported.

What are holy conversations? Theological questions are posed and the discussion may be to explore the possible answers. While most congregations will have core beliefs such as a belief in Jesus, the peripheral beliefs are open to discussion. Examples of these questions are: "Do you think that babies are born good, sinful, or a blank slate? What do you think happens when we die? Why do you think that bad things happen to good people? What do you think heaven is like? Do animals go to heaven? Does God answer prayers? How do we explain the seeming dichotomy between evolutionary theory and the story of creation as recounted in the Bible?

We designed "faith circles" as a place to talk about one's faith, to share one's answers to theological questions, to challenge each other, and to witness to divine intervention. Answers that are different from one's own are to be respected. The leaders of faith circles are those who have learned how to articulate their own story in order to encourage others to share theirs. We often talk about "defining moments" as those personal experiences of faith that led us to challenge our current perspectives on religion, but such challenges move us to spiritual growth. Defining moments often arise out of the dust of a personal crisis or tragedy, when we realize that our faith is not sufficient to be able to help us to "make sense" of what we are going through and therefore we need to revamp our faith, which often leads to different answers. The emphasis in faith circles is that faith is not a "fixed" factor in our pilgrimage but, like a circle, has no beginning and no end.

Faith circles not only allow for holy interactions, but they are "practice" for being able to do evangelism. We are not used to sharing our defining moment. Most of us do not even know what one is or how it relates to our faith. Yet, what "witnessing" entails is a personal experience of encountering a "defining moment" that either gently nudged us or forced us to challenge the inadequacies of our faith and take our spiritual growth to the next level. One of the most significant changes that this process leads to is a change in one's image of God. Some people will hold to a judgmental, punishing divinity who is just waiting to exert his wrath on unsuspecting people trying to live good and decent lives. Defining moments summon us to revisit such images of the Divine to experience the compassion, strength, and support that Jesus sends to us through the Holy Spirit.

In faith circles, we emphasize developing empathy. We view empathy as the "highest" level of holy interactions. It is one level to identify with someone's defining moment and say, "I've been there. I know what you are going through." It is quite another to say, "I can only imagine how painful that must have been." When we put ourselves in someone else's situation and try to imagine what it must feel like to be in that situation, we are developing empathy. Empathy allows us to enter into their world and to discern what they need in order to heal from their experience and to witness to the way in which the Holy Spirit works through us to provide that healing. We also believe that the incarnation of the Divine in Jesus is God's act of empathy that lets us know that God knows what it is like to be us.

I once preached a sermon "What Not to Say at a Funeral" because people tend to say rote things in a receiving line that they do not
believe and are not a source of comfort to the bereaved. Some may believe "everything that happens, happens for a reason." but there is
usually no immediate good reason for their grief. When individuals
are experiencing pain, they tend to be walking receptacles of pain.
Thus it is a natural reaction for others to create emotional distance
from them so that they do not experience the pain of the grieving.
What sets organized religion apart from other social organizations is
that it equips people to be able to provide empathy, to enter another's
world, and to imagine what it is to be them at this moment in order
to be instruments for the comfort of the Holy Spirit.

OPPORTUNITIES FOR HOLY INTERACTIONS

When I first arrived at the church I serve, I was amazed to find that
the women of the church had continued the tradition of the "circles,"
each named after a woman of the Hebrew Bible. These groups of
about eight to ten women meet at each other's homes for fellowship
and are organized around the umbrella of the "Ladies Benevolent
Association (L.B.A.)." These women have developed holy interactions among each other and model how small cell groups can be developed in the church to meet our spiritual needs for relationships as
well as engage us in social justice. (For instance, they gather together
to make supply kits with various items to be sent overseas.)

After the church began to attract women of the postmodern generation, the L.B.A. attempted to attract them to join the fellowship
group. They put announcements in the bulletin. They rearranged the
meeting time to accommodate working women. But still the young
women did not attend. "What is the matter with women today?" they
wondered. "We are close and supportive of one another," they witnessed. The women were frustrated because they perceived that the
younger women were not valuing the holy interactions that had been
so meaningful for them. If the women of the L.B.A. were offended, it
was not until their postmodern pastor also didn't want to attend their
meetings that they were *really* offended. So instead of insisting that the
younger women be involved in the way that the "older" women had
engaged in holy interactions, we invited the younger women to form
their own group. This group functions quite differently, but it serves
to meet the same spiritual need for relationships.

Traditionally, programming was the avenue for promoting holy interactions. These programs include Bible study, women's and men's groups, and committees. Programs as a concept are not changing, but there is a movement among healthy churches toward redesigning what these programs offer and accomplish. Whereas Bible study may offer an opportunity for conversation about daily life among the modern worshipers, it is not likely to appeal to the postmodern believers, who may be more interested in a course on global religions. The postmodern believer is not interested in serving on committees because of the way in which they function: individuals are chosen to be on a committee by a powerful group in the church known as the "nominating committee" and then committed to this group for three years, which may or may not coincide with the length of time needed to fulfill the committee's function but is convenient for the nominating group. The aura of most churches is that one waits to be invited to participate, rather than signing up based on what interests and motivates the individual. Often people are asked to serve on several committees because of lack of overall motivation within the system. Who wants to be asked to do something because they couldn't find anyone else?

There are two kinds of cell groups in a contemporary congregation. The first are natural cell groups that often develop based on "like" cultural groupings such as age, gender, economic circumstances, or ethnic background. When I attend a clergy gathering, I naturally flock to other women, who are often gathered together in the corner. One may observe this phenomenon at fellowship hour as well. Natural cell groups tend to form based on cultural grouping, presumably because those in a specific group share similar interests and often share similar views about how they perceive the organization should function. In a cultural environment where there are few opportunities to gather with like people, especially for those who have newly immigrated to this country, natural cell groups are an important aspect of holy interactions.

Contemporary congregations also design cell groups for the purpose of intentionally bringing together a group of people who would not otherwise have the opportunity to interact with each other. For instance, our advent workshop is designed so that an individual entering receives a passport that is color coded, and that individual travels from room to room (in each room engaging in a different spiritual exercise) with other individuals with whom they might not necessarily interact if the church structured itself after other social organizations. Once a month, the deacons also sponsor a breakfast based on color coding, and one sits at the table with others with the same color code. In this design, parishioners get to know other parishioners outside of their cultural grouping.

As a multicultural, multiethnic church, these designer cell groups are an important aspect of our congregational functioning. Prejudice, as a free-floating evil force that is projected onto a cultural grouping, often determined by the media, can be exorcised through holy interactions. Once an individual forms a spiritual connection with another individual from a different cultural grouping, then the strength of that connection keeps the demon of prejudice out. Projection only works on people we hardly know. The surprising grace of this process is exhibited when individuals realize that they share much in common with another individual from a different cultural grouping. Designer cell groups function for the purpose of uniting people, whether randomly through color coding, or based on interest, such as through a program or Bible study.

Youth groups that limit themselves to social interactions will have difficulty sustaining involvement. The view on the outside by the postmodern believer is this: "Why would I join a youth group? I have a car and I can go to the movies with my friends. I don't need a youth group leader bringing me bowling on Sunday afternoons." An indicator of a church's emotional health is the functioning of its youth groups. Churches that do not have youth groups because they cannot attract youth or do not have a leader who is willing to take on this ministry need to re-invest their energy and money into prioritizing their youth ministries. An effective youth minister is one who does social activities in order to foster holy interactions among the youth—to provide a place where the youth can openly share their faith and practice doing so in order to evangelize other youth.

TRANSFERRING HOLY INTERACTIONS

The way in which people relate to each other in the context of a religious organization should be held to a higher (healthier) level of functioning than is tolerated in other social organizations. This higher level refers to the closeness of members' emotional and spiritual connection to others in a trusting environment in which they can share of themselves, their struggles and joys, and talk about the ways in which God is present in their daily lives. We view this level as "higher" because it ultimately functions to bring us closer to God. The pilgrimage of spiritual growth is dependent upon "healthy interactions." Thus, pastors need to be well skilled on these patterns of relating and aware of their own patterns of relating, and they must be able to distinguish healthy patterns from dysfunctional ones. Pastors must also be able to teach the congregation (through preaching) how to transform dysfunctional patterns of relating into healthy patterns.

When organizations become depressed, it becomes more difficult to maintain functional patterns of relating. Energy is often generated by focusing on the pastor's performance. Someone notices something that the pastor has neglected to do or something that has not been done to the level of expectation. One person mentions this to another person at coffee hour and through this conversation they become energetic, wondering, "Do other people feel the way we do?" They might gather a group of people together, who may or may not actually perceive that there is a problem worth addressing, but they become caught up in the whirlwind of negative energy—and when there is no other energy circulating within an organization, any kind of energy is experienced as a welcome relief. I find that people jump on the bandwagon just because it feels good to have a cause to fight. Accessing energy makes a congregation feel alive, whether that energy has negative or positive results, destructive or creative. When few opportunities to access energy present themselves (in terms of social justice), the congregation will create their own.

Healthy interactions among parishioners produce healthy organizations: healthy organizations naturally transfer holy interactions into the community. An individual learns healthy patterns of relating and practices these patterns in all aspects of congregational functioning. When patterns are dysfunctional, the congregation themselves encourage individual members to transform these patterns into healthier ways of relating, not only with each other, but with family, friends, neighbors, and colleagues. In so doing, they will also experience spiritual growth as they re-image their faith and perception of the divine realm. When parishioners are equipped with these healthier patterns of relating, their loved ones connect the dots and realize that it is their participation in organized religion that is responsible for the change. They then want to experience this transformation themselves. This is the essence of evangelism.

three | evangelism

The second day in seminary, we were encouraged to sign up for field education interviews to be "student ministers" in a local congregation. Twenty-two years old and right out of college, I had not set foot in organized religion since I was sixteen when my parents had divorced and my mother had felt shunned by the congregation. In the beginning of my third and last year, I pleaded with the director of field education, "I am never going to be a parish minister" and so why should I have to do field education in a church? The Holy Spirit resolved the first issue and First Baptist Church of Newton Centre, Massachussetts resolved the second.

Instead of being a student minister *in* the church, I would be what we would call a "lawn minister." The church had been experiencing a "problem" with youth gathering outside their magnificent gothic structure and "hanging around." They were really nice kids. After warming up to me and feeling comfortable (I was only a few years older than them), they shared with me their life, their struggles, their faith. I got good at sharing my defining moment, the story of my faith. I spoke of the predicament that I was in, that I had not been in a church for several years, but now I was in seminary. They would laugh and say, "You don't seem like the type!" (It has taken me many years to realize that is why God called me.) When the time came for me to go *inside* the church and preach, they all wandered in. It was my first experience as an evangelist.

I have prayerfully searched for a different word in this chapter, other than "evangelism." In the mainline church, we associate this function with knocking on doors, being pushy and obnoxious, and threatening damnation and hell. Even the evangelicals have renamed their movement, "postevangelical" in order to move away from the idea of "selling" the church and having to persuade, convince, and manipulate individuals to want to become part of organized religion. Evangelism simply means to speak of the gospel message, to say, "Hey, I have some good news," and to share our defining moments. Evangelism is the practice of holy interactions *outside* the church rather than containing that spiritual energy to inside the church.

I am convinced that evangelism is not the only issue. When resources become scarce, there is a natural tendency for those inside the walls to hoard what little they have left. I refer to this affectionately as the "beaver" mentality. Those inside focus their energy on damming up their "water" in order to conserve these resources. Whether or not an actual time of famine is impending is irrelevant, for the perception in organized religion is often, "We'd better save for a rainy day so that if something happened to the church building, we can reconstruct it (even with insurance)." The fears expressed about this famine focus on finances, "Where is all this money to fund all these projects going to come form?" Or the view is on the organization itself, "Shouldn't we take care of our own?"

But there is a deeper fear that lies just under the surface of this "damming" response. When I hear things like, "Don't you think we already have *enough* people?" I sense a fear that if other people come into the church there will be a power struggle for what little energy is circulating within the congregation. If the modern worshiper can articulate this fear it sounds like this: "Will I still be close to the pastor?" or "Will I still be the chair of the nominating committee?" or "What if someone comes into the church who plays the piano better than I do?" Fear of being replaced, fear of losing power, fear of new ideas and change, fear of having to share the pastor's caring (and if the pastor is the only caring person in the congregation this is a *real* fear): all of these forms of fear raise the level of the congregation's anxiety about engaging in evangelism. There might also be a fear that the pastor is not happy with those who were currently "the congregation" and is trying to design a contemporary congregation by replacing the old congregation with a new one.

To encourage people who are not used to taking risks, a religious leader must help them to discern a good reason to change their present behavior. We affirm that the congregation is good at welcoming others once they are within the church. They are warm and friendly (like every other church). But those who come into a church on their own represent a certain personality type and if we only welcome one kind of person we are practicing segregation (which in our multicultural church is the buzzword that makes people want to do whatever is the opposite). We spoke frequently about how we need to be about something "bigger than ourselves," and that the church exists for a reason beyond itself.

In a church, a community of faith, that good reason should reflect what we believe God is calling us to do. Jesus' commission in Matthew 28:19–20 is often cited as the biblical foundation for evangelism, which is of interest to us, because the word translated as "nations" is actually the word for "ethnicities." Segregated churches base their evangelistic efforts on bringing more like people into their religious organization, but that is not what the commission is calling for. If we narrow our evangelism to those who would come to a church on their own, then we are going to attract people like us; if the postmodern generation is missing in that collection, then we have not fulfilled that commission, even in a megachurch. The idea is not to collect a bunch of like people, but a diversity of ethnicities, as evidenced by the use of the Greek word *ethnos*.

Another reason to engage in evangelism is to produce karmic balance. When a new force of energy is introduced into a system, it energizes and is energized. The concept of "people flow" means that a constant flow of people coming into a church and going out is a dynamic that keeps a congregation functioning in the healthy mode. When a stream ceases to flow, the water builds up and turns "yucky." People flow is like a stream of water flowing clearly and sparkling when the sun reflects upon it. This flow also reduces the incident of beaver activity because no one individual or group of individuals does the same task for very long, but are encouraged to equip one another. The ministry is equipping the disciples, not any given task itself.

In the glory days, hanging out a sign that said "Everyone Is Welcome" was an effective strategy for evangelism. People driving by would notice the sign, and if they were new to the community and loyal to their denominational affiliation they would say, "There it is, the Congregational church we are looking for!" But those days have come and gone. The postmodern believer may not have been raised within the church and may have little, if any, emotional connection to the church of their parents' upbringing. The only way they are going to cross the border from outside to inside is because someone inside gives them a good reason to do so. Unlike their parents, whose "good reason" was because their family already went to church, entering the church is a personal choice for the postmodern believer. This observation alone raises the bar on evangelism to a whole other level.

Whereas the modern worshiper joined a local church because it welcomed them inside the church, the postmodern believer will make the decision to attend a church on the outside. Thus, evangelism is a two-part process, from A to B and from B to C. A represents the invitation or the "good reason" for attending a church. The most likely good reason is because someone from inside of the church witnessed to a defining moment of divine intervention and the postmodern believer seeks that same experience. Sharing our faith is the very essence of holy interactions. The postmodern believer may not wait for an invitation to this experience but may ask, "Can I come too?" B represents the process of assimilation, which I will refer to as "welcoming." C introduces the process of equipping the new disciple for ministry.

POINT A TO POINT B: INVITATIONAL EVANGELISM

For several years I volunteered as a global village work camp leader for Habitat for Humanity, traveling throughout Central America to build houses alongside those who would live in those houses. I was as changed from the experience as the people who were the designated "recipients" of our help. Some of those families who received a Habitat home were active in their local church and others were not. But all were curious about why we would raise money, get on a plane, be separated from our families, and travel to a remote section of the world, where mosquitoes pass on malaria, just to help them out. I came to realize that what they most wanted to know was what was within us that would motivate us to do this. As we shared our faith, our own experience of having to be dependent on others for assistance and our need to give something back, we were often then asked if there was such an organization in their walking distance.

When I had moved into the community where I now serve, I had attended a band concert at the high school and sat two chairs away from another parent with whom I got talking. When I shared with her that I was new to the community, she invited me to attend her church. I affirmed her invitation and explained that I had been called as the pastor of another church. I then asked her what was the source of her inspiration to invite me to attend her church and she responded, "Because I know it's hard to meet people in this town. It's my job as a Christian to make sure that no one feels lonely in a new community." I thanked her for her offer of fellowship and went back to the church to ask if we were also inviting people in the community to worship with us. The response was that we were sending letters to people who had purchased homes. We needed to expand our efforts.

Our church also does not view invitational evangelism as an attempt to get people to go to our church, but to *a* church or faith community. As supporters of organized religion, it is important that we know something about the other religious organizations in town that may be a better fit for a postmodern believer. While we are Christian and believe in Jesus as the incarnation of God, we acknowledge that others experience the divine connection in other images and expressions of worship. Our congregation is interested in global religions, the customs of which, as mentioned previously, are often tweaked into the practices of our worship service. Therefore, our approach to invitational evangelism is not promoted as a way to get bodies into our particular church, but to connect the postmodern believer to organized religion.

The contemporary approach to marketing can essentially be summarized as "witnessing to the value of a product." Some companies are hiring the "average" consumer and asking them to invite others to their home to use the product and then comment on whether or not they like the product. For instance, one woman had everyone over to her house for a barbecue. When her friends liked the way in which the hamburgers were cooked, she shared with them the product on which they had been cooked. While I am quite aware that there is a movement away from applying marketing principles to invitational evangelism, we are used to sharing with friends when we like a certain product. In a consumer-driven culture where people often "church shop," it may still be an effective way of making known what the church has to offer and that what the church has to offer is unique.

We also did not limit our invitational efforts to the postmodern believer, but also sought to bring back parishioners (modern worshipers) who had stopped attending church on a regular basis. Our assumption had been that the reason they had stopped coming was because they were angry, hurt, or upset about something that was happening in the life of the congregation. At the time, it felt easier to ignore these people, especially if they were high maintenance, and hope that they would go away quietly. We were afraid that if we called or visited with them, we would get an earful. But surprisingly, if they had felt emotionally hurt from an incident within the congregation, the feeling had long passed and now was replaced with feeling hurt that no one from the church had reached out to them, as if no one cared. It was much more likely that the reason they had stopped attending was because they themselves were going through a major crisis and they thought that their absence would be noted and people would reach out to them.

I often run into parishioners whom I have not seen in church for quite awhile, and they say to me, "Oh, I am so embarrassed, pastor. I have just been too busy to make it to church. I should get back into the swing." For years, my response would be, "I understand that you are busy. It's alright. I hope to see you soon." I was letting them off the hook and enabling them not to make an effort to be in church the next Sunday. What was I thinking? I know part of me dislikes confrontation and so I avoided it because I didn't want them to walk away angry. Now, I say, "I am embarrassed that no one has come to your house and dragged you out of bed. You should never be too busy for God and your friends at church. We miss you and expect to see you on Sunday." We have become lax in our expectation that parishioners should attend worship every week and be involved in ministry during the week.

POINT B TO POINT C: WELCOMING EVANGELISM

The postmodern believer is now showing interest in the church. They have moved from point A to point B. What are the variables at point B that will attract the postmodern believer to move to point C?

I do not think it matters how many hands a postmodern believer shakes. It is more important that they make significant relational contact with a few people. Congregations need to make every effort to appear "open" to forming relationships with new people, rather than closed, closely knit communities. When the postmodern believer observes holy interactions but does not participate in them, it makes them feel as if they are intruding into someone else's space without an invitation. The bond that encircles a congregation can appear to an outsider as a difficult one to traverse through. Fellowship, or holy interactions, can be our best strategy for evangelism; but they can also be counterproductive when they do not welcome the outsider into the flock. No one wants to stand at the gate and observe all the sheep grazing together.

It is often noted that the modern church appears to function as a private country club, delegating the role of pastor to activity director. Even though this observation may give the church a bad rap, it may also witness to the strength of the bond that is produced by the holy interactions that take place there. People in the church are close with one another and that is a good thing. I do not know too many country clubs that offer such emotional closeness where people can talk about the intimate details of their lives. But the contemporary congregation will make every effort to function as a *public* place of worship, where the flow of who is in and who is out is not only fluid, but the boundary lines themselves are blurred.

I compare welcoming evangelism to how families welcome visitors into their living room. If I am expecting company, I usually clean. I want my home to look nice. I want my visitors to feel comfortable in the furniture and leave with the impression that the home is nicely decorated, contemporary (and I live in a Victorian home), and well maintained. I serve food from a new recipe or that perhaps involves some effort for me to put together (and I am not a cook). It is that same approach that we need to take when it comes to "curb appeal" in designing contemporary congregations. As Tom Bandy says, "Property is a window into the soul of the church."[1]

Throughout history, human beings have worshiped their gods in sacred places that were set apart for such purposes. It was within these sacred spaces that their faith developed and their connection with the spiritual realm was experienced.[2] The modern worshiper has a relationship with the building as sacred space. They take much pride in its sanctuary, landscape and architecture. As a blessing, sacred space invokes an awareness of the presence of God and provides space for sacred rituals. "I feel God when I enter this place," says the modern worshiper. But such invocations can also function as obstacles to "church merging" by which two congregations come together in one church building in order to share resources. Most congregations would rather die than close their doors and move up the street. This attests to the strength of this connection with the physical building. As has been the approach of this book, we work with the tide, not against it.

But the postmodern believer does not have that same history with the church building and thus does not share the same emotional connection with it. Whereas the modern worshiper sees the white rectangular box style of Congregational churches as "beautiful and traditional," the postmodern believer sees it as "old fashioned." The modern worshiper views their steeple perched on top of the church as a symbol pointing to heaven and everything divine, while the postmodern believer comments that it looks like a phallic symbol. (A side note to those congregations who are currently thinking about replacing their steeple in order to attract the postmodern believer; nothing could be more counterproductive. Invest the money in another strategy presented in this book.) Most church starts are opting against the boxy rectangular configuration with a steeple in favor of something with a wider chancel, moveable seats and large clear glass windows overlooking a pond.

In chapter 1, I spoke of the energy of resistance being directed against changes made in the worship service. When leaders begin talking about changing the appearance of the physical building, we are likely to encounter a second wave of resistance. "Why would you want to change this beautiful building?" the modern worshiper asks. But changing the setting by redecorating, putting an addition on a building, applying a new coat of paint, updating the kitchen, and/or installing a new carpet in the sanctuary can in itself generate new energy.

I would suggest that a group of members get together to assess "curb appeal" by taking a tour of the church after a prayer for a new perspective and attempt to see what others might see when they come into the building for the first time. We are more likely to "see" things in any physical space—a home, church, office building—when we are developing a relationship with that space. The longer we have had a relationship with a physical space, the less likely we are to notice both its strengths and its imperfections. This is especially true when trying to sell one's house. Prospective buyers tend to notice every little imperfection and want it corrected before they buy the house. The owner often responds, "Oh, that never bothered me. I hardly noticed it."

The group is commissioned to take note of every object in every room and determine which of three lists it should be placed on. The first list is designated for those physical objects that invoke the divine presence, that makes one feel connected to God. The second list is for those physical objects that historically made others feel a sense of connection to the divine (and therefore may be retained for their historical value). And the third list comprises those objects for which no one in the group can recall a reason why they are there, where they came from, or their religious meaning. Some in this group loved this "trip down memory lane." But most were amazed at how many objects in the church building belonged in the third group.

The first list contained "the keepers." The communion table, the gold cross, the Bible on the communion table—all these were deemed both historical and contemporary symbols of the Christian church. The second group of physical objects raised the most debate, so we did not discard them nor sell them at our yard sale (the fate of objects in list number three). But we removed them and they remained in the attic for one year. If they were missed by a group of people, then they were reinstated. Interestingly, few people missed any of the items, and only after several months did someone say, "Hey, wasn't there a picture on that wall?"

When congregations purchased the series of Warner Sallman prints in the 1950s, they were contemporary to the modern worshiper. When most Christians image Jesus, they are imaging the famous portrait of Jesus by Sallman painted in 1950. He also painted Jesus knocking on a door, praying in the garden of Gethsemane, and so on. I often say that they must have been on sale because so many churches purchased them that it is unusual to find a church that doesn't still have them in their collection. They are out of date, however, because they image Jesus as a member of the white middle-class dominant group, which cannot possibly be an accurate representation of Jesus' ethnic background. Imaging Jesus in this light also contributes to the prejudice that we image God with features corresponding to those in the dominant culture.

Another object that generated much discussion for us was the board counting the bodies in the church, last week and one year ago. The congregation was proud to report this number, because the numerical growth was an indication that our efforts were successful in attracting the postmodern believer. But what did it say to them? We are only doing this to collect more marbles than the church down the street? Are we playing the numbers game and seeking to supersize our church or are we genuinely concerned about the spiritual health of our community and are looking for ways of strengthening the people's ability to access divine power in their moment of need? Objects in the church communicate messages to a visitor. It is extremely important that we know what the message is.

Special attention should be paid to the outside of the building. As any real estate broker will tell you, individuals make impressions about the property in their initial first glance and then weigh everything else they see against that initial impression. Curb appeal measures at what level you begin; if the building starts with a low impression, it has to more than make up for that impression inside. Landscaping and a well-chosen color freshly painted on the façade send a message: we care about our physical building and we care about the people inside. We hope that the people on the outside will feel invited and welcomed. Churches that are functioning on a limited budget may rethink painting the inside of the sanctuary in favor of painting the front of the church. Also, it may have been "in" twenty years ago to hang a wreath with plastic flowers on the door to create a warm country feeling, but today it is "out."

The color scheme of the rooms also needs to be evaluated. I have lived in my house for ten years and some rooms I have painted several times. Now, I happen to like to paint. But my point is this: the quickest shift from contemporary to traditional and back again is color, and yet color is also one of the, if not the most, significant factors in a physical building that determines its contemporary status. Neutral colors are often thought of as "timeless," but contemporary colors at the time of this writing are bold and bright. I am not suggesting that a congregation paint their sanctuary bright blue, but a congregation might hang a brightly colored quilt or banner in a prominent place to offset neutral colors on the walls.

As a part of the process of designing curb appeal, I would recommend that the congregation ask a few postmodern believers to tour the church. They may be a well of fresh ideas with respect to color and which physical objects communicate to them. Once postmodern believers begin becoming active in the church, this process may be repeated as there may be objects that were overlooked and are functioning as obstacles to attracting other postmodern believers.

What do we replace these out-of-date objects with? I appeal to both the modern worshiper and the postmodern believer to show their artwork. We show paintings, quilts, banners, and drawings created by those in every age group. On Saturday mornings, we have "art classes" and have taught watercolor painting, quilting, flower arranging, and more. These classes have provided us with a steady stream of artwork to view, and we change the artwork on a regular basis (so that people actually see it). Also, because we are a multicultural church, we encourage multicultural images of the Divine.

The purpose of evangelism is to make disciples of Jesus who are committed to living the teachings of Jesus and using that teaching as a guide to social justice and action. Thus, objectives to discipling these believers are assessed for their value of achieving this goal. If a congregation insists on persuading the postmodern believer to join organized religion, this should be viewed as an objective leading to the goal and not the goal unto itself. If the postmodern believer joins a church and there is nothing for them to do and the church does not have anything unique from other social organizations to offer them, they will simply fade away even after they have formally joined.

In contrast to years ago when an individual who formally joined a religious organization was making a lifetime commitment, the concept of commitment has changed in postmodern culture. Fewer postmodern believers will formally make a commitment to their life partner through the covenant of marriage. They fear divorce. It is also considered socially acceptable to live together. One no longer commits oneself to an employer/organization to work there until retirement. In the postmodern world, there is less of a focus on a long-term commitment, but this should not be viewed as being less of a commitment, for it only reflects the transitory nature of our culture.

In contemporary congregations, there will be less emphasis on formal church membership. Historically, the individual has had to attend membership classes in order to learn how the church functions, that is, "the way we do things around here." But this approach circumvents the design of a contemporary congregation where those coming into the system are encouraged to participate in the design of that system. Alternatively, the traditional approach is to have a designed system that is not subject to change or revision. Membership classes tend to be a rubber stamp of this traditional approach and, therefore, I recommend that they be revamped into discipling classes that focus on the objectives discussed in this section. Such classes are taught by both modern worshipers and postmodern believers and open to all in the congregation. They do not focus on the way that the congregation functions, but they share stories, hopes for the future of the church, past celebrations, and ongoing social justice projects and educational programs. The classes share "what we have been doing up until now and we hope that you will join us for all the exciting things we hope will unfold in our future."

The current discussion on discipleship emphasizes "high commitment" to the congregation's functioning. But invoking this level of energy will often attract those with an addictive personality, who already have histories of substance addiction, and who can thus replace one addiction for another. While we *should* be attracting those with addictive personalities, we should be providing a therapeutic environment through which they practice moderation. In modern functioning, one was either a committed member or a peripheral member (who came only to worship), but the contemporary idea is to energize a "faithful member" who contributes Holy Spirit–driven gifts to the functioning of the contemporary congregation. I advocate that discipling evangelism helps the individual to assess a moderate level of energy directed toward the organization with the intention of using that energy to be directed outward, to social justice and to improve their psychosocial functioning in their interpersonal relationships.

Most religious leaders are not in a position to be able to assess which disciples are manifesting addictive behavior toward the church's functioning and which disciples are just enthusiastic. Those who attend worship one week and then volunteer for three task forces the following week probably have some issues. Discipling does not mean enabling the addictive personality to rechannel dysfunction for the benefit of the church. A skilled leader will refer that person to a professional who can help them address their addiction in order to free them from this dysfunction. An addictive personality who overengages energy into the congregation will expect too much in return and will be left feeling angry, frustrated, and disappointed with one more transitional object that has failed to make them feel better.

Furthermore, individuals who are willing to make a high commitment to an organization tend to be those who are seeking power: those who seek power tend to hoard it. These people overfunction for the congregation, which only reserves enough energy for others to underfunction. In contemporary congregations, one person can only serve in one position or on one task force. The "multiple hat" syndrome is a symptom of dysfunction in a congregation, masking depression. A church that appears to function at "peak capacity," where every role is filled, communicates to the postmodern believer that there is nothing for them to do and therefore they are not needed.

In the attempt to move away from the either-or mentality that pervades the thought process of the traditional church, I would suggest we encourage "medium commitment" rather than low commitment, which currently characterizes the traditional church,[3] or high commitment, which is often characteristic of new or emerging churches.[4] Medium-commitment churches do not have to encourage worship attendance because people want to come on their own. Instead of going from giving a very small portion of their income to sustain the church's resources to giving everything they have, medium commitment means to tithe 10 percent of income. As stated elsewhere, the verdict is still out as to whether or not high-commitment churches can sustain that level of commitment and energy from their adherents over long periods of time.

In a newly forming medium-commitment relationship, expectations should be clearly stated. The congregation needs to custom fit what they expect from their disciples and their disciples need to articulate what they expect from the organization. When someone says to me, "I want to do it and I expect nothing in return" that translates to me as "I want something but I don't know what it is and I reserve the right to decide what I want at a later date." Conflict is likely to arise when that person comes to "cash in" on their return when I might not be able to deliver. While there are costs to discipling, there should also be immediate, intrinsic benefits (and hopefully those benefits are of a spiritual nature). One of the most effective ways of evangelizing the postmodern believer is to encourage them to be involved in a congregation that is active in social justice. They will receive the benefits of feeling good about themselves and strengthening their connection to the spiritual realm.

Postmodern believers will come with their own ideas about contemporizing the congregation as well as ways that they want to be involved. The church that says, "This is what we need you to do," or "These are the committees that have a few openings left that we were unable to fulfill at our last nominating meeting," are setting themselves up not to attract the postmodern generation. Rather, the church asks the postmodern believer, "What do you believe you have to offer us?" They probably will not know because they haven't had an opportunity to discern these gifts. A response may be, "Maybe we could work together to discern your gifts. That's how I found out what I was good at to be a disciple of Jesus."

In the past, a new member of a church was expected to sit by the sidelines and watch and learn how a congregation functioned and then follow the lead. The modern worshiper who expresses this pattern may say to the postmodern believer, "Well, we should do it my way. After all, I've been a member here a lot longer than you." The surest and quickest way of launching a battle between the two groups in the church, this is to be avoided at all costs. Such warfare could lead to a split in the church, the postmodern believer on one side, the modern worshiper on the other. It may even lead to a schism in which the postmodern believers break away from the modern worshipers and begin their own church (and this is not what the postevangelicals mean by a parent church).

The organization's willingness to share its power equally distributed among modern worshipers and postmodern believers will be the most important single factor in making the transition from the traditional church to a contemporary congregation. Length of membership is often used as justification for hoarding power. Discipling evangelism is about making both the modern worshiper and the postmodern believer disciples of Jesus together. Once the postmodern believer becomes part of the organization and attracts other postmodern believers, this artificial dividing line between those who are modern worshipers and those are who are postmodern believers will slowly fade away and, instead, those who believe in Jesus will become a new group, "disciples of Jesus."

But there is another key to transition from the distinction between the two groups to assimilate into one at this point in the process, and that is the issue of multiculturalism. Segregated congregations will not naturally attract persons from other cultural groupings. The church whose efforts focus on a specific "cultural grouping" of postmodern believers will also sabotage any effort to contemporize the congregation. The postmodern believer who walks into a segregated congregation— segregated either in terms of ethnic background, economic circumstance, sexual orientation, ability, gender, or age—will probably not return. They will assume that there is a level of comfort in their segregated status. It is for this reason that a congregation without young people is less likely to retain a young family who attends worship for the first time. While initially this is a challenge for the church, attracting one or two young people who are encouraged to engage in evangelism will set the process in motion.

Because the postmodern believer tends to be accepting and honoring of those from diverse cultural groupings, the congregation who practices prejudice against a specific cultural grouping will not attract them. Congregations who are struggling with their prejudice toward gay and lesbian persons by "inviting and welcoming" them into their midst in order to change them or "heal" them of their homosexuality are communicating to the postmodern believer that they want to retain the right to choose who is "in" and who is "out." In the contemporary congregation, the boundary line is lifted from the secular and the sacred, from the private and the public, from exclusive to the inclusive. We invite and welcome everyone. That is what Jesus teaches us to do.

four | equipping the disciples

I can still see her coming through the receiving line to say something nice about the sermon. Helen Elden faithfully attended worship each week. She never married. She lived very modestly in an apartment building located in a problem-infested downtown area. When she died at ninety-three, she was still on three bowling leagues. Few people in our community have much money and so it is not unusual for someone to be buried in "potter's field" in Boston. But because Helen had been good friends with the mother of our church's administrative assistant, she offered to pay the expenses for her burial. A few months later, an estate attorney contacted the church to tell us that Helen had left some money to the church. I breathed a sigh of relief, hoping that I could at least return the funeral money. After the estate went through probate, we received a check. It was for a million dollars.

For months, I agonized over the question, "Why didn't Helen tell me how she wanted the money used?" I recalled our last conversation when she was in the hospital. She never mentioned anything to me about the money. I went over that conversation again and again in my mind. It took us some time before we realized that Helen trusted that we would know what to do with it. For quite awhile, we had been talking about all the ways that we could equip the disciples of Jesus to do ministry and trusted that when we were ready to do this, the money would somehow be there. This fall we will open "The Helen Elden Center for Ministry." And by the way, when I die and go to heaven, my one question for Helen is not what she wanted us to do with the money, but "What was the defining moment for her in the life of our congregation when she decided to give that money?"

What do we envision that the Center will do? It will serve as the home base to equip the disciples for ministry; a kind of school or neighborhood seminary. We will offer courses on multiculturalism and opportunities for holy interactions between ethnic and racial groupings. (Some people thought that it should be a center for racial relations, but we have all agreed to incorporate multiculturalism into its wider mission.) The Center will pay professionals whose specialty will be to teach disciples with a variety of methods. Some people learn best through a classroom setting with a teacher who imparts knowledge. Others learn through reflecting on their experience in small groups with people they trust. Still others learn through reading the books in our extensive library. Our mission is to be sensitive to the variety of ways that people learn to discern their gifts and be empowered to go out into the community and use those gifts.

Our philosophy of "equipping disciples of Jesus" differs from that advocated by those in the postevangelical movement who perceive that becoming a Christian in and of itself makes one able to function as an effective caregiver. Rather, we believe that, with a little more wisdom and guidance, through studying the scriptures, role playing care-giving interactions and learning what helps and doesn't cause further hurt can serve as a foundation to equip disciples to do the ministry of Jesus. We observe that many Christians with "good intentions" (and even some with not so good intentions) intervene to help and make the situation worse. For instance, when a disciple encounters a situation of domestic violence or child abuse, they should be equipped with a strategy to intervene in such a way that this family gets professional help.

For a congregation to alleviate its depressed mood, lift its suppression of spiritual energy, and become a vital congregation, all disciples need to be equipped for ministry, including the pastor and all parishioners (both the modern worshiper and the postmodern believer). This design is distinct from the traditional church, which views the pastor as the one who is trained to do the ministry. In the contemporary congregation, pastors are still the ones trained in a professional seminary to do ministry, but they pass on this expertise to the leaders, who pass it on to others. Thus, the ministers of the congregation are the congregation itself, which honors the idea of "ordination": the servant to the servants. But most pastors are still functioning according to the traditional model and, therefore, will need to be convinced to change and try a different mode of functioning. Just as pastors advocate that their congregation should change, so the congregation will need them to change.

THE SHIFTING ROLE OF CLERGY

Most pastors were trained to serve congregations interacting with modern culture. Equipped with courses in systematic theology, church history, and biblical studies, after seminary we were ready to preach and teach the masses sitting on the edge of their pews and hanging on to our every word. We were warned that being a minister was a time-consuming profession that came with certain "sacrifices": we were not to put ourselves first before the parishioners we served. Even when very tired and overwhelmed, we were to work as many hours as possible in a week to be considered faithful servants of Jesus. Often we had little interaction with anyone who was not connected to the church. We were to function with little emotion as models of "healthy" professionals. Because I cry easily and often from the pulpit, I felt I had failed miserably to uphold such professional standards.

That we had to go out to the community and bring other people in was beyond the scope of my ability. That we would serve tired, depressed, chronically anxious congregations who would see us as "the last hope" for breathing new life into dry bones was not what I had signed up for. That a congregation would blame us for the current state of the church rather than view it as a developing problem that originated in the glory days with the greatest pastor a church ever had was something I had no preparation to argue against. Let's face it. Those who serve as clergy in a postmodern culture were trained to serve in a modern culture, and serving a traditional church in a postmodern culture is fraught with tension, anxiety, and frustration. And because most clergy function as emotional "sponges" for their congregations, they carry these feelings around with them as if "carrying the world on one's shoulders."

But we accepted the call and responded to the challenge with the intrinsic reward that we would serve in a "high status" profession. In the modern world, being a pastor was upheld as a "professional call-ing" that invoked respect, dignity and prestige. Alongside law and medicine, being a pastor requires three years of education, and the Masters of Divinity was considered among the "classics" of all masters degrees. But in our postmodern culture, clergy are looked upon with suspicious eyes. With the recent disclosure of sexual abuse by clergy, we are to be distrusted until we can prove ourselves worthy of being trusted. Perhaps no other profession, in our postmodern times, is more devalued than that of pastor.

It is understandable, then, that clergy too often cling to those in-side the church who still look at us with eyes of admiration. The modern worshiper idealizes the pastor as if seated at the right hand of God. Our personal self-worth (and professional esteem) needs the modern worshiper to continue this idealization, because its alterna-tive, devaluation, raises our anxiety. As the congregation engages in evangelism, the pastor may be anxious about who will be brought in and whether or not they will subscribe to the value of idealizing the pastor. Most clergy will attempt to sustain this value by trying to please everybody, doing it all, visiting every visitor on Sunday by Monday morning, and being the center of attention in the worship service. The pastor's personal need to be idealized "hooks" the pastor to enable the traditional congregation to decline in numbers rather than to turn around and design a contemporary congregation that at-tracts the postmodern believer.

We refer to this as "pedestalizing" and the opposite is referred to as "authenticity." The current movement is toward being "the authentic pastor" who is "down the earth." First of all, these idealizations are "projections" and pastors cannot control projections to the extent that they think they can. Being ourselves and not seeking to be someone we are not is a basic developmental schema that is not unique to being a parish minister, but to all human beings. Authenticity is often used as justification for forming friendships in the church, which is contradic-tory to what some view as our professionalism as pastors. We are either pastors or friends, but not both (see chapter 7). Splitting perceptions into idealizing or devaluing is one more example of the "either-or" mentality that is symptomatic of chronic anxiety. In a healthy congre-gation, most parishioners will know the strengths and weaknesses of the pastor, and the weaknesses will not be held against them. Instead, what the pastor does not do well will be done by someone else.

Many pastors were the "gatekeepers" in their family of origin (myself included). We controlled the flow of information from one family member to the next and appeared to be the seat of all knowledge because we would collect this information and then decide to whom it was dispersed. Knowledge comes with power and control. So many of us become "control freaks" who perceive that almost everything that needs to be done in the life of the church will be done better if we do it ourselves, because no one else will do it as well as we do it (so we think). Pastors also convince themselves that they need to know everything that is going on in the congregation. As in a family system, when we do not know, we feel out of the loop and, therefore, not in control. Part of the reason why pastors feel that they are the circle of all knowing (which extends to also having the one right answer to any theological question) is because they have been raised as gatekeepers and have exchanged this personal role for a professional function.

I confess that for years I thought that everything that should happen in the church should happen around me. I was the center of attention or, in professional jargon, I was the "catalyst" who controlled the movement of the spokes of the wheel. When something happened "behind my back" I became paranoid that they were out to get me. I was afraid of letting go, because to do so would risk that the whole might fall apart, or at least the church would crumble piece by piece right to the ground and it would be my fault. One time I was really paranoid, so afraid that those who were gathering were plotting to overthrow my power in some way; it turned out that they were planning a surprise birthday party.

For those who struggle to feel power in other relationships and often feel powerless, this power is seductive. Churches distribute power to anyone who walks through the door and is willing to help. The more desperate the church is to find "workers," the more likely they are to attract people who are seeking that power. Parishioners relate to the pastor as a representative of God: because God is imaged as all powerful, that power is projected onto pastors. Those who feel helpless or powerless in other relationships want to be close to the pastor, who radiates power. When the pastor allows them into this inner circle, they feel powerful and will support the pastor in order to remain in that circle. This dynamic functions to reinforce the boundary line of dominance and marginalization operating in segregated churches, because some people have power while others have less.

The second shift in the pastor's functioning in the contemporary congregation will be the move away from the expectation that the pastor functions as a generalist who is supposed to be good at just about every aspect of congregational functioning to that of a specialist who is encouraged to pursue their own gifts for ministry. This shift serves two purposes: first, it gives room for disciples of Christ to do ministry in their area of specialty, and second, it renews the pastor's imagination, creativity, and energy to specialize in an area of ministry that brings them fulfillment. In postmodern culture, most professions are shifting from generalization to specialization as our knowledge becomes more specialized. Being a generalist today involves knowing more than did being a generalist in the modern world several decades ago. Functioning as specialists sets us free from feeling frustrated and anxious and allows us to capitalize on our strengths and improve those skills. It also allows us to find the time to practice spiritual meditation and to strengthen our relationship with God.

When I was leaving one of the churches I served, the youth group made me a quilt and they each wrote a message to me. One youth wrote, "To a woman whose talents helped us to realize our own." His words of affirmation ring whenever I am tempted to overfunction and do it all. In my own discernment process, I have come to accept that my gift is to function as "a liturgical artist." The Greek word *liturgia* means "the work of the people." In traditional worship, we refer to the lay person who reads the scripture as "the liturgist" but the word in Greek has a broader meaning: to embrace all the ministry of the church, "the ministry of the disciples." The leader who creates opportunities for ministry, orchestrates creativity, and prays for the Holy Spirit to descend by preaching, teaching, modeling, mentoring, and confidence building does so not only based on skill, but with an artistry that inspires others.

Equipping the disciples for ministry has allowed me to have the time, energy, and flexibility to continue my education. Instead of trying to be all things to all people, I can now focus on what I am good at and learn to do it better. I enjoy taking courses at the local seminary and this allows me to get to know other clergy in the area. It also expands my mind to continue to develop my skills, which renews my energy. Continuing education and time are part of my job. The church pays for me to do this and I schedule to take courses during my work time, rather than perceiving continuing education as an extra at the bottom of a long list of priorities. This way I model for the congregation that becoming a disciple of Jesus is a lifelong learning process by which we are continually discerning our gifts for ministry. What will sustain the energy of the contemporary church, compared to the traditional church with its declining resources, is that we believe that equipping disciples of Jesus is a continuous process.

We believe that gifts may be part of our genetic code, that is, given to us when God creates us in the divine image. But gifts can also be nurtured, developed, and strengthened through our interaction with culture. Theologically speaking, God continues to create us throughout our lives. Those gifts that others affirm that we do well are the gifts that we tend to want to develop and that will naturally energize us for ministry. Some people are undoubtedly hardwired for certain behaviors, but we operate under the assumption that with love and support, as well as training by professionals, each of us can engage in a specialty ministry that is important to the life of the contemporary congregation. We see these gifts as "treasures in earthen vessels," which should not be hidden but be a light onto others. As Jesus teaches, "Let your light shine before others so that they may see your good works and give glory to your Father in heaven" (Matt. 5:16).

I will have little to say in this chapter about the difference between the modern worshiper and the postmodern believer (and the subtext of the book is to show how both have the same spiritual needs and thus can function together in one faith community). Both the modern worshiper and the postmodern believer desire to be equipped as disciples of Jesus. We have found yet another point of connection between the two. A congregation that attracts postmodern believers but cannot retain them needs to have in place something for them to do, whether as disciples of specialty ministries, task forces, and/or social justice (chapter 5).

SPECIALTY MINISTRIES

Every disciple of Christ has a gift for ministry bestowed upon them by the Holy Spirit. "Now there are varieties of gifts, but the same Spirit; and there are varieties of ministries, but the same Lord; and there are varieties of activities, but it is the same God who activates all of them in everyone. To each is given the manifestation of the Spirit for the common good" (1 Cor. 12:4–7).

If everyone is blessed with a gift for ministry, then the church's reason for being is to help people to discern the gifts that equip them for ministry within the life of the congregation and for "the common good" on the outside. Discerning those gifts is itself a specialty: parishioners often can neither perceive what their gifts are nor how to apply them for ministry. The pastor plays an important role in this process, developing a close relationship with parishioners in order to get to know them and to help them identify these gifts. Some parishioners will need to be "built up" to have the confidence to use their gifts and be affirmed when those gifts are well used. One of the most important aspects of my job as pastor is to serve as a mouthpiece for God when I say to a parishioner who has used their gift for ministry, "You are my daughter, my beloved, with whom I am well pleased."

In the traditional church, the process of discernment has often been based on one's interest or the job one does to produce income. If one is interested in teaching Sunday school or leading the youth group, the assumption is that that person may have a gift for teaching children and adolescents. The nominating committee functions to fill "spaces" on the various committees. Sometimes because they are often representative of the modern worshiper who is invested in sustaining the status quo, they fill committees with other modern worshipers who share their investment. They get anxious about asking a newer parishioner to serve on the diaconate because that newer parishioner does not have the experience of having first served on another committee and "proving" that they are not too radical and will not try to rock the boat. In small churches, parishioners may know each other well and be aware of each person's gift for ministry (although I view discernment as a specialty itself), but in large churches using this design to link gift with ministry is like rolling the dice: you might just happen to ask the person with the gift to serve on a committee that will need that gift, but the chances are against it.

In the traditional church what tends to happen is that someone engages in a specialty, becomes frustrated because that is not their gift, and yet is encouraged to continue to do it. The traditional congregation fears that shifting people in and out of ministries will cause a "unfilled space" on a committee or task force or in the Christian education program. The fear of unfilled positions leads to the multiple hat syndrome, when one individual in the church has to function in more than one specialty. If one already does not feel that the first function is producing spiritual energy, then the nominating committee may have to twist one's arm to serve a second or third function in the congregation.

In a healthy congregation, more than one person wants to be the youth minister, but the one who is chosen is the one who has already demonstrated that they can be trusted with the youth and have a particular gift for relating to young people.

Some congregations are using inventories for discerning gifts; but this may simply determine interest rather than gifts. We view past experience as the best predictor of future behavior. If a disciple has a history of being the one to whom everyone turns in times of crisis, then that disciple is probably good at crisis intervention and should be encouraged to pursue further training in that specialty. If a disciple enjoys public speaking and witnessing to the power of the Holy Spirit, that person should be encouraged to join the worship team. Alternatively, those whose past behavior does not indicate that they have a specific gift should be pointed in another direction. If a disciple has never invited a friend to church, they might not be the best person to lead the evangelism team. If a disciple cannot balance a checkbook, then encouraging them to manage the church's finances might not be the best idea. One of the reasons why people are leaving the church is because their gift for ministry is either not accessed or has been made to fit into another specialty of ministry.

If a gift is a seed that produces the fruit of ministry, spiritual energy will be nourished in the organism. When seeds are not sown in solid ground, the birds come and eat them. Dried up branches cause a disconnect with the vine. Individuals may leave the church feeling angry and frustrated, losing faith and feeling spiritually unfulfilled. When we feel our gift from the Holy Spirit is used to be a disciple of Jesus, we feel closer to God and that connection is strengthened. As Jesus says, "I am the vine, you are the branches. Those who abide in me and I in them bear much fruit, because apart from me you can do nothing" (John 15:5).

There are a variety of specialties. One of the most popular is visitation. The training covers subjects such as depression, suicidal tendencies, death and dying, alcohol and drug abuse and dependency, familial violence, and soon. Visitation training equips the disciple with skills for confrontation, comfort, caring, and compassion as well as referral. We emphasize that when a disciple feels that they are practicing beyond their field of expertise, if they feel that "this is more than I can handle," they should refer the person they are visiting to either the pastor or to another professional. The church provides phone numbers of professionals that specialize in any of the problems just listed and who can objectively intervene. The role of the disciples is to form holy interactions that set the foundation for intervention to happen in the first place. Often someone will admit that they have a problem to a disciple and that disciple then refers them to a professional counselor and/or a self-help program. The disciple initiated the first step in the process of healing and recovery, the turning point or defining moment, and may witness to their own defining moment as a way to provide hope.

Another new model that is emerging is "a crisis intervention team." This team is prepared to minister in a crisis situation, which is often emotionally charged. When a family is faced with needing to confront a member whom they believe is drinking too much and they want to encourage that member to enter a rehabilitation center, they may call the crisis intervention team. (The team may consist of only two or three disciples so as not to overwhelm the person who is being confronted.) This team is equipped for crisis situations as a specialty ministry. Some of them learn skills of caring confrontation. Others learn how to minister to those who are experiencing grief and may be called immediately following the death of a loved one or when a spouse requests a divorce.

Along with visitation and crisis intervention, other specialty ministries include teaching and organizing programs. Those with teaching gifts lead Bible study, often around a particular contemporary subject. We also offer adult education as a series that includes subjects such as the history of the church, the Protestant reformation, the history of our denomination, the symbols of the church, and the foundations of Christian faith. Organizers are those whose specialty is planning events for the church, such as a gospel choir concert or a fund raiser for our new organ. We also have a music program that teaches young people how to play the drums or guitar to play with one of the praise bands.

We have also realized that each of us accesses our spiritual energy to use our gifts at different phases of the change process. For example, I enjoy shopping for the fabric to make a quilt and designing the pattern, but as I begin to piece, my energy often plummets as the process moves into the stitching phase, which I find tedious. Similarly, I have found that I am good at the design phase of contemporizing a congregation but I depend upon other disciples to sustain it into the "equilibrium" phase.[1] As change is a process of design, plan, implementation, and equilibrium that sustains those changes, we need to discern at what point in the process our gifts can be best utilized.

TASK FORCES

There are two major differences between specialty ministries and task forces: 1) specialty ministries require gift discernment and ongoing training for ministry and task forces are formed based on interest, and 2) specialty ministries have no beginning and end whereas task forces are task-specific and time-limited to accomplishing the task. Specialty ministries may equip one person to do that ministry for an entire lifetime, but another person may emerge as a leader to equip other disciples. Task forces gather together a significant group of people to both engage in social justice (the subject of the next chapter) and equip disciples while they are engaging in the ministry itself.

A common response to specialty ministries by the modern worshiper may be, "Who is going to do what the committees used to do?" In the design of the contemporary congregation, which, at least initially, blends the traditional with the contemporary as a transitional model, committees evolve into task forces. The committee that doesn't perceive that it does anything becomes equipped with specific tasks that need to be done to sustain the church's functioning—for example, the trustees who put together a budget to be presented an annual meeting for approval. While task forces themselves may require specialties, the movement is away from using this specialty long-term, as in a person who is good at finances serving on the board of trustees or finance committee most of their life.

Task forces are only are in existence for the time necessary to complete the task: from brainstorming options, choosing a plan of action, debating alternative plans of action, agreeing on a plan of action, strategizing about its implementation, and then assigning responsibility for implementation, implementing the plan, and then evaluating the implementation and ongoing functioning. When the task is completed, those on the task force move either into a specialty ministry or onto another task force.

HOLISTIC PRACTICES OF SELF-CARE

Postmodern culture emphasizes that we need to take care of ourselves in order to be able to take care of others. Thus the contemporary congregation will design itself to provide opportunities for disciples to practice self-care. Even though we are spiritually energized by being disciples and using our gifts for specialty ministries, that spiritual energy also needs to be directed inward to nurture the self and our spiritual connection to God. We encourage parishioners to engage in daily exercise through aerobic activity such as running, walking, and lifting weights. In the area surrounding our church building are many walking paths, and we teach ways to meditate while on those paths, practices borrowed from Eastern religions. We also recommend healthy styles of eating and guarding against obesity, which has become an epidemic among our children. Basically, we believe that caring for ourselves physically is also a reflection of the ways we take care of the body of Christ.

We also encourage disciples to spend time in activities that are "alone time" as karmic balance to times spent developing holy interactions. Jesus interacted with his disciples but he also spent time in places where he could be by himself. In this alone time, we suggest that parishioners exercise their "creativity" through a hobby such as quilting or through another artistic expression. On Saturdays, we run a series of creative lessons. We have taught cooking classes, watercolor painting, floral arranging, beading, and more. Our church is also the meeting place for the New England Woodcarvers Association. Then, once a year, we hold an art show throughout the church and exhibit everyone's creativity. (We also charge admission and the proceeds go to support Action Against Poverty, an organization that gives money to women in Nigeria to begin their own businesses.)

Our strategy to equip disciples to do the ministry of Jesus focuses on body, mind, and soul, all interconnected to produce spiritual energy; the more connected and healthy is each, the more energy we are able to access and the greater able we are to spread the love of Jesus. As Ephesians says, "But speaking the truth in love, we must grow up in every way into him who is the head, into Christ, from whom the whole body, joined and knit together by every ligament with which it is equipped, as each part is working properly, promotes the body's growth in building itself up in love" (4:15–16).

five │ social justice

"And what does the Lord require of you but to do justice, and to love kindness, and to walk humbly with your God?" (Micah 6:8)

Mainline liberal Protestant churches thrived in the 1960s and 1970s, promoting civil rights, supporting the Jesus movement, advocating for peace in the midst of war, and so on. As a social and religious organization, a public institution, and a forum for dialogue and action, the church functioned to energize its congregation to go out into the community and engage in social justice. Religious leaders not only functioned as motivational speakers, but pointed to traditional sources of authority, such as scriptural interpretation, in order to discern the church's position on political, economic, and social issues. Prayer served as the energizing force to send forth the servants into the community as instruments to change the current policies to make them more in line with the interpretation of scripture. The modern worshiper was a hippie at heart who believed passionately and faithfully that what they were doing was making a difference in this world.

What happened?

Since the 1980s, the mainline liberal Protestant church has been silent and passive on issues of social justice. It fears controversial conversations might split the church because "We are not all going to agree." In its vulnerable and depressed state, the congregation is afraid to talk among one another, not only about their faith, but about how that faith translates into action. Most people are only willing to disagree when they are in a solid relationship. Avoiding any conversation for fear of infighting sustains the church's depressed state. Elsewhere, I have spoken about how the church's silence on violence enables violence to continue.[1]

Whether it be concern for the poor or those suffering oppression in some other way, there must be *something* that every church can find as a rallying point. I am convinced, wholeheartedly, that every church feels passionate about a specific issue of social justice that might not be articulated but may be known by every parishioner as they live and dwell in a specific community. No one is immune to witnessing our social plights and no Christian could be numb to the suffering that they cause. While we may not all agree on what causes those social issues, we are likely to agree on a method of intervention.

The postmodern believer views the church as conservative on most social issues. This is because the conservative mainline Protestant church has been quite vocal about their perception of these issues. People outside the walls of organized religion do not know that some churches may be conservative and others liberal (if there is such a thing) and so they assume that all churches think the way that the vocal ones think. Many conservative churches have voiced opposition to the civil right of legal marriage for gay and lesbian persons, and so the postmodern believer assumes that all churches share that perspective. If they didn't they would voice their opposition. It is a cultural norm in the dominant group to openly disagree with what others are saying; silence conveys support.

The cultural pendulum is swinging back; what was popular in the 1960s and 1970s is now popular once again. Retro design in clothing, music, furniture, and more is considered "contemporary," whereas, a decade ago, it was "old fashioned." During the Vietnam War, peace protests were held in every shape and form, and as we confront the war in Iraq, similar protests have emerged. Protestors today use similar strategies of social justice that were used in the generation of the modern worshiper. Additionally, there are mass protesters who are voicing opposition to current political policy, especially concerning the issue of immigration and policies affecting patrolling our borders.

This swing presents a window of opportunity for the church to return to its status as a mover and shaker, a shaper of contemporary culture, a voice in the wilderness preparing the way, a major player on the field of economics and politics. During times of unrest, culture has historically depended upon religious organizations as a source of authority. Now, more than ever, culture needs organized religion to be the light in the darkness, a guide in the wilderness, an instrument of peace. But only those organizations that have been influenced by culture will culture invite to the discussion table. The influence must be reciprocal; only when organized religion enters into the world of culture and reflects its contemporary trends will culture perceive that organized religion should have a voice.

To assess the current level of the church's functioning with respect to social justice, the influential interaction between church and culture, we may ask, "If this local church were to close tomorrow, would it be missed by its cultural environment?" If the answer is "no," then this is another indication that the congregation is probably in a state of depression. When an organism or an organization becomes depressed, it is a natural survival strategy to turn inward and focus on self-preservation. This natural tendency, however, must be resisted in favor of turning outward. Even if an organization can access energy within itself, that energy runs the risk of suppression if it has no outlet in which to regenerate itself through action. When this happens in a religious organization, leaders hear, "If we can't take care of ourselves, how can we take care of others?" A response to this question may be, "The only way I know to take care of you is to equip you to take care of others."

The way to care for those within the organization is to energize and equip them to take care of those in their cultural environment. Turning from an internal focus toward the external surround energizes the organism to look beyond itself. By doing so, the organism is able to begin the process of healing its depression. The more excited parishioners get about their ability to "make a difference," the more energy they access within the system. They not only bring others back with them, for social justice is another aspect of invitational evangelism, but they energize those within the congregation who may still be a little reluctant about venturing into the public arena to do ministry. This cyclical process of karmic energy feeds a congregation desperate to see the fruits of their labor yield a harvest. When parishioners become enthusiastic toward a cause, that enthusiasm translates into energy, and that energy catches others into the net of enthusiasm.

Equipping the disciples for social justice is a specialty. We do not assume that everyone already knows how to do social justice just because it is often associated with "holding protest signs" on our church lawn or hiring a bus to go to the statehouse to make our voice heard when legislators are voting on a bill. In our culture, there are many "do-gooders," but there is a difference between what they do and what we do as Christians. Social and human service professionals are also well trained to do their function in this area, but often their intervention focuses on helping the individual rather than confronting social forces, for example, the economic policies that cause the problems that the individual is experiencing. The congregation's function, then, is to address social issues on their systemic level by confronting social organizations, policies, and programs that sustain the dualism of dominance and marginalization.

Briefly stated, our culture functions by maintaining a centralized power base that hoards most of the world's resources. A boundary exists around this power base, which is protected by the interests of those within the circle to keep others out. Almost all of the rest of society exists on the perimeters of this boundary line and are referred to as "the marginalized": those who live paycheck to paycheck and/or do not have access to health insurance. They struggle to access the minimum amount of resources that are held tightly by those in the dominant group. The problem is defined as "the unequal distribution of power" between the two groups and the solution includes policies that serve to redistribute the resources more evenly.

Here is more good news: both the modern worshiper and the postmodern believer want to engage in social justice. Social justice represents a point of interconnection in the process of contemporizing organized religion that transcends generational lines. The modern worshiper recalls the energy that was accessed when they were active in the protest marches and rallies, the sit-ins, and the anti-organization stages of the hippie, student protest, and civil rights movements. They can mentor the postmodern believer in similar strategies for social justice today. The postmodern believer may also serve as a motivator for them to return to these glory days and, in turn, they serve as a motivator for the postmodern believer by sharing these days and the difference that they made.

Social justice begins with the way in which a social organization models itself as a just organization. For instance, the social organization that advocates for human and civil rights but does not marry gay and lesbian persons may be perceived in the community as inconsistent, as in "Do as we say, not as we do." Many liberal denominations have taken a stance on this issue, but the local church has not supported this stance, and yet the denomination still advertises the local church as if they do support these civil rights. Thus, the congregation must design itself as a "just social organization" where the criteria for "just" is the equal distribution of power among the disciples of Jesus for ministry, which was discussed in the previous chapter.

EGALITARIAN POWER STRUCTURES

The root of all social problems is the complexities of economics, and therefore almost all of our contemporary social issues revolve around politics that determine economic policies. The unequal distribution of opportunities and resources between the dominant and the marginalized groups accounts for the dichotomy between the haves and the have-nots. In contemporary culture, there is a third category of "sort-of-haves" who may have a job but no health insurance. While the children of the haves can access money to attend college and the children of the have-nots are often eligible for financial assistance, those honoring the Protestant work ethic may fall between the cracks and may not be able to afford to attend college. Economists predict that the gap between the haves and the have-nots is widening. A few of the sort-of-haves are entering the haves but most sort-of-haves are crossing into the have-nots.

The traditional church has historically functioned to mirror these societal dynamics. The traditional church was designed to function with a sole pastor who was the nucleus of the power base in the church. All decisions went through him and he attended all committee meetings, ensuring that this way of functioning prevailed. Given that pastors function as the representatives for God, the omnipotence of the divine is projected onto pastors and pastors are often viewed as all powerful. The historical traditional church functioned under a two-tier system: the pastor had power and was the dominant group, and everyone else was in the marginalized group and should do whatever the pastor said they should do. In more recent history, the traditional church has functioned on a three-tier system. The pastor is among the most elite with power, then there are those who surround his power, the second tier. All those who are in the congregation and have little power represent the third tier. Most congregations continue to function under this three-tier system, as do most other social and political systems in our culture.

It seems evident that this three-tier system, which supports an unequal distribution of power between those in the dominant group (who include the first two tiers) and those in the marginalized group (who represent the third tier), is no longer working. Those in the third tier are drifting away from the church because there is no power available to them to access in order to engage in social justice. Meanwhile, those on the second tier are revolting against the pastor's power and complaining about those in the marginalized group. The modern worshiper observes, "Those people come to church and put two dollars in the plate and then never do anything to help." There is a gap between the "workers" in the church and everyone else. This gap is filled with resentment from both sides. The dominant group in the church complains that the marginalized group "uses" the church and does not participate, and the marginalized group feels that there is no room for participation because the dominant group holds tight to their positions and power.

How to convince the dominant group to let go of some of their power and share that power with the marginalized group is the essence of "liberating the oppressed," which has been the historical understanding of the church's position on social justice. When we convince pastors to share their power, by empowering religious leaders to equip disciples to do ministry, then we begin the process of liberation. We also find that all benefit by this more egalitarian power structure. The pastor does not feel overworked, as has been a major complaint among clergy serving the traditional church, and the congregation is not depressed because of its suppressed energy. Everyone wins. When a social organization makes a shift in its thinking and mode of functioning, and when this shift is perceived as positive by all, the organization models to other social organizations a more just way of doing things.

The design of a contemporary congregation will be to distribute power based on function, that is, power is assigned to those who need the allotted amount in order to fulfill the function that they serve. For instance, a treasurer of the church needs to be able to write checks to pay the staff but should not be able to decide how that money is spent. In the contemporary congregation, the distribution of power is disbursed to accomplish a specific task that has been assigned. In the traditional church, power is assigned based on length of membership, ability to give to the stewardship campaign, or because that individual lies within the realm of the dominant group with respect to cultural grouping. Historically, white, middle-class men have made the decisions for our social organizations.

During the shift, pastors will continue to be religious leaders and function to empower other leaders. The postevangelical movement, in response to these issues, advocates for a leaderless congregation where all disciples do the ministry of Jesus.[2] While this may be a grand attempt to shift organized religion from functioning as a hierarchical power structure to an egalitarian one, it represents the either-or mentality that this book advocates against. Leaderless social organizations do not remain leaderless for long. Those who are used to being in charge in other social organizations will naturally emerge to take over. Those who are most likely to emerge into these positions of leadership are white, middle-class, able men and women. Because they represent the dominant group within our culture, they are used to having power; those in the marginalized group are used to allowing them to do so.

A good leader is one who makes every attempt to empower others in an area of specialty. Leaders who are able to discern a disciple's gift, inspire the disciple to use that gift, and then affirm the ways that the disciple uses that gift for ministry will be needed in the contemporary congregation. While pastors should be educated in seminary, leaders in the congregation may be educated and equipped for leadership by the pastor. "Leadership is about being led."[3]

MODELING MULTICULTURALISM

In *Becoming a Multicultural Church* (Cleveland: Pilgrim Press, 2006), I explored how multiculturalism honors race, ethnicity, gender, age, sexual orientation, economic circumstance, and ability. A congregation that excludes one of these groups is practicing prejudice, and the congregation that practices prejudice will have difficulty attracting the postmodern believer.

Postmodern believers may have attended colleges where affirmative action policies were honored and they are accustomed to relating to people who are from other cultural groupings. In the eyes of the postmodern believer, the segregated church is not only a red flag of prejudice, but reeks of being "old fashioned." After visiting a segregated church, they may say to a friend, "I didn't know there were any relics of segregation left in our society!" They conclude that the church does not change because it likes itself that way. The postmodern believer is tolerant of this way of thinking, just as they are of more progressive thinking, but that doesn't meant that they want to attend or support a social organization that functions this way.

Segregated congregations are at such a disadvantage of attracting the postmodern believer that this may be the single variable that sustains congregational depression and keeps the energy of attracting new people at bay. Congregations naturally attract like people, and so segregated churches will attract those from their segregated groupings. Meanwhile, as culture becomes more "multi" as a result of immigration and policies that allow diversity in public display, the church that does not try to be in sync with these cultural changes will not survive. Churches that draw exclusively from people like themselves will soon find that they have a smaller pool from which to fish.

Because I resist the church-within-a-church model of church growth, that is, having a "youth service" or any other form of segregation, I also advocate against "renting" space to another worshiping group. This feeds into our thinking that members of the church "own" the church. When they are resistant against change, they will say, "But this is my church!" That mentality also enters into the discussion of immigration, when people say, "This is my land!" Congregations do not "own" the body of Christ, nor have exclusive rights to control the sacred space of the Holy Spirit. As a public institution where everyone is welcome, we do not segregate any aspect of congregational functioning, whether that be worship or holy interactions.

Although the Christian church lags behind other social organizations in its quest toward multiculturalism, it is in a unique position to practice holy interactions among persons from diverse cultural groupings (as I spoke about in chapter 2). Such cultural trends as urban vitalization, which tends to bring together those from diverse cultural groupings, is a positive step forward, but all we ever hear about through the media are the problems. The church could be a forerunner in showing culture that racial relations can be developed into holy interactions, when people come together to worship God in Jesus and to be spiritually connected to one another.

Environmental Stewardship

Other signs of an outmoded congregation are the ways in which they deal with environmental issues. Recycling programs for trash, converting trash to treasure, and designing a green program are all ways that the contemporary church practices stewardship of God's creation. If the church has access to land, growing organic vegetables and plants models for the community good stewardship. And when the harvest is plentiful, it may be an opportunity to invite the neighborhood to a large picnic in the backyard of the church. The coffee that is served at coffee hour may be purchased through a "fair trade" vendor. Fair trade coffee, which is grown by independent, usually indigenous growers using environmentally sound practices, can also be made available for parishioners to purchase to use at home. The contemporary congregation advocates for the rights of humans and animals, and if it discovers that it has bats in its belfry, it sponsors a bat relocation program.

One of the most wasteful modes of functioning in the traditional church is the monthly newsletter. To pay a secretary to write, copy, collate, and fold several thousand pieces of paper and sort by zip code for a third-class mailing is not a productive use of time, energy, and resources, even less so in our day of computer technology. The contemporary congregation will use the Internet as its main instrument of communication. I might suggest that an e-mail newsletter go out weekly from the church that is less than one page and divided into three sections: a pastoral note, upcoming events, and joys and concerns.

HOLY INTERACTIONS WITH THE POOR

Historically, the church used to be involved in a direct relationship with the poor. The pastor would gather money from those in the congregation and then go into poor communities and preach to the poor that if only they repented from the causes of their poverty, usually related to morality, they would no longer be poor. The pastor would then distribute the money to the poor. This way of voicing concern was misdirected to the victims of poverty, not to the social organizations that function to sustain poverty.

The current movement is away from blaming victims for their own problems. We no longer believe that tragedy befalls people solely because of their own actions. From a systems perspective, we are realizing that we are part of the problem if we are not working to promote a solution. Those in the dominant group often say, "I'm not oppressing anyone," and deny that they are part of the problem. This is why religious leaders have to teach social justice; it is not just a matter of empowering congregants to go out into the community to make a difference. Both denial and guilt (guilt often is under the guise of denial) are obstacles to promoting social justice and suppress energy for action. Blaming the victim, denial, and guilt have all contributed to a mode of social justice that creates emotional distance between those who help and those who need our help.

The story of Job illustrates this emotional distance. Job, the victim of life's tragedies, has three friends show up who create a disconnect between themselves and Job. They profess a theology that says, "You must have done something to be in this present situation, and your actions have offended God." In this way, they function under the misperception that as long as they do not do whatever they assumed that Job has done, then such tragedies cannot befall them. But what stands out for us is that the very first verse of the book characterizes Job as "blameless and upright." The moral of the story is that Job did nothing to bring this upon himself, just like the poor are not directly responsible for their own economic circumstances. If Job could end up in the marginalized group, then so could anyone else.

The traditional church is also depressed because it has sustained its dominance by creating emotional distance between itself and the poor. Social justice is practiced by writing checks to support programs such as Neighbors in Need and One Great Hour of Sharing. We are asked to share our resources under the assumption that those in the church are in the dominant group and have resources to share (which may or may not be true), and that our mission is to share those resources as good stewards of what God has given to us. We do not seek to relate to the poor in order to access our energy to make a difference in their lives. We do this simply to meet a need, enabling us to remain within our own comfort zone, preserving the status quo of the hierarchy, and keeping the marginalized entrenched in their marginalization. Writing a check does not access energy and thus has no direct impact upon congregational depression. If one exerts little energy into social justice, one will receive little in return.

Emotional distance is also sustained by handing out money via the congregation (which is really just a leftover remnant of the pastor passing out the money in the poor community). In the traditional church, the poor approach the church office, often looking for money to support drug or alcohol dependence, and the pastor, out of the goodness of their heart, disburses money. The problem with this practice is that the poor are well skilled at spreading the good news that the church still operates under this outdated practice and can be a good place to seek a "free lunch." Most clergy realize that this is not working when they hand out money the next day and see a line of the needy outside the office with their hands out. Because this was done for so long, contemporary congregations are still asked directly for money. I will often say to someone who asks me for money, "If this story ends with you asking me for money, then let me tell you up front that I do not give out any money. If you are not looking for money, please sit down and I would be happy to hear your story, but I don't want to waste your time and energy."

The church needs to reflect upon its practices of social justice to ascertain whether or not it enables, directly or indirectly, the problem to continue. Our social service welfare system is designed to keep poor people from revolting against those who hold the resources. Economists do their research to develop a numerical amount of money that the average family of four needs to sustain basic human needs. If, for instance, that number was grossly insufficient and a leader emerged to stage a revolt against the dominant group and mobilize the poor, it could throw our economy into crisis. The same theory is behind how we determine what the minimum wage should be. Instead, the church should work to promote education as a vehicle to prevent poverty. The church should offer programs such as English as a Second Language (ESL) that are practical ways to help the immigrant, who is likely to become poor in this country, to overcome the language barrier.

Soup kitchens illustrate a transition between emotional distance and relational social justice. Those serving the food would often make conversation with those who were in line to receive it. Some even ventured to the table and sat with the poor to share a meal. But soup kitchens to serve food to the "poor" often did not respect the dignity of the poor, and the poor often may be shamed to be in a soup kitchen line.

The movement today is toward relational social justice—social justice in which those who are in need and those who want to help work side by side. Many churches are offering community meals open to anyone who wants to eat with others. These meals tend to attract the poor and lonely; but, in a multiracial community, they also tend to attract those who are "curious" about the culture of others, and many will come simply to "test" the culturally diverse food and will subsequently form relationships. We ask different cultural groupings to prepare the food, but there is a core group who are responsible for the weekly community meal. As we get to know some of the regulars who come to this meal, we invite them to help us to prepare the meal for others. This way, everyone takes turns helping.

The contemporary trend of social justice is to form a relationship with those whom we seek to help. One of the best examples of this trend is the way in which Habitat for Humanity functions. I have worked as a global village leader for the past twenty years and led several groups abroad. A family selected to receive a house has to put in five hundred hours of sweat equity on another house after being chosen but before their own house is built. When our church sponsors international trips, to pick up and pilgrimage together for a length of time, we feel good about our own involvement in social justice. Whenever I have brought a group of people from our church on a trip to build a Habitat house, we all come back enthusiastic for mission. We bring that energy back into the system and energize that system for social justice.

A THEOLOGY OF SOCIAL JUSTICE

One of most important lessons we learned about social justice is that no one wants to be on the receiving end of being helped for very long. This may be one of the major reasons that elder persons do not want to go into a nursing home. To reach a phase of life when we are dependent upon others for our basic needs does not invoke energy nor make us feel very good about ourselves. Human beings have a natural inclination to want to be helpful, and when we are affirmed for doing so, we feel good about ourselves and we access spiritual energy. Thus, when we are in a position to give, we work to empower those who are receiving to be able, in their turn, to give something else (which may not be to give financially, but to give of themselves). We believe that this is what Jesus means when he says, "It is better to give than to receive" (Acts 20:35).

Another important insight with which we function in our congregation was expressed recently to me in this way. "In our church, no one is considered any better than anyone else and, if that is true, then we'd better hang in there for each other." We believe that God blesses us with the opportunity to share what we have with others and that everything we have is a gift from God to be shared, not to be hoarded. We also believe that most of our gifts are not tangible resources, but gifts of caring, compassion, and understanding that flow from the heart.

We believe that every person we meet may be the incarnation of God, the return of Jesus. We design our functioning to treat others with dignity and respect because it would be just like God to show up in a person whom we would least expect to be the incarnation. Our theology of social justice comes from the passage in Matthew 25:35–36 when Jesus says, "I was hungry and you gave me food, I was thirsty and you gave me something to drink, I was a stranger and you welcomed me, I was naked and you gave me clothing, I was sick and you took care of me, I was in prison and you visited me." Those who engage in social justice will ask, "When was that?" and Jesus said, "Just as you did it to one of the least of my brothers and sisters so you did it onto me" (v. 40, my own translation).

six   **l i f e - c y c l e   r i t u a l s**

Years ago, a young mother called the church requesting a baptism for her child. I asked if she would either like to meet in my office or I could come to her home, whichever felt more comfortable for her. She responded that she would like me to come to their home, so we scheduled the visit. But the day of the visit, she called me to let me know that she and her husband had decided to have their child baptized as a Catholic, so that if the child later decided to marry someone who is Catholic, the two would be able to get married in the Catholic church. I wished her well. The next morning I received another call from her wondering where I was the night before as they had been expecting me. Surprised, I replied, "I'm sorry. I understood that you had decided to baptize your child Catholic." "Yes" she said, "I want you to baptize her Catholic." And I responded, "If I baptize your child, *your child will be Protestant.*"

Afterwards, when I had regained my composure, I began to wonder if I had missed an opportunity to attract the postmodern believer. Don't we believe, as Christians, that we baptize into the Christian religion, rather than as Protestants, Catholics, or Greek Orthodox? I had missed an opportunity for a teachable moment with a postmodern believer who was simply looking for organized religion to say, "Yes, we love your child as a child of God and we commit ourselves to you in holy interaction to help raise this child in the Christian religion." To what extent do we change our rituals just to attract the postmodern believer? Is there not a fine line between playing the numbers game and staying true to the historic collective meaning of these traditional rituals? Do we change the rituals themselves, their practice or meaning, to make them contemporary in form?

Interestingly, we found that the postmodern believer respects the traditional rituals of the Christian church with the same intensity as the modern worshiper. We had discerned yet another point of connection. Life cycle rituals, the naming and blessing of a child, weddings and funerals, are practiced, in some form, in almost every ancient and contemporary global religion. Self-proclaimed "atheists" will frequently seek out rituals at a church, especially baptism for their child, "just in case it's all true." Parents still want their children blessed. Brides still want to walk down the red-carpeted aisle in their long, white, flowing gown. Most of us still want our loved ones to pray for us when we transition from this life to the next.

Life-cycle rituals are a window of opportunity to engage the postmodern believer in organized religion. It is often at this point of connection that the postmodern believer makes contact with the church to request this ritual. But interestingly, it's traditionally designed to be "done" by the pastor, with little opportunity to develop holy interactions with others. Everything we have to offer that is unique is hidden from view when a bride and groom prepare for a wedding and walk down the aisle. The pastor is also usually the only contact when a family requests a funeral in the church for their loved one. Essentially, the postmodern believer who requests a life-cycle ritual sees the church in its traditional mode of functioning— the pastor who does it all, rather than witnessing to all the changes that have been made to become contemporary. Therefore, a contemporary congregation needs to shift, not so much the way we perform these rituals, but the way that we engage those who request them.

In the traditional congregation, life cycle rituals are perhaps the point of most frustration for the modern worshiper in terms of attracting the postmodern believer. We stand up during a baptism and promise to help to raise this child in the Christian faith and then we never see the child again. To deal with this frustration, some congregations have begun offering these rituals only to those who are church members or affiliated with the church through a member. My understanding of why some churches practice this type of exclusion is to encourage commitment, but when we feel rejected by a group of people, we are not likely to then want to make a commitment to them. At the same time, neither is the revolving door at the front of the traditional church doing much to attract the postmodern believer.

Perhaps as a result of this mass exclusion, fewer postmodern believers are seeking out these rituals in a church setting. The contemporary movement is toward doing baptisms in the backyard, weddings on the beach, and funerals at funeral homes. This may demonstrate how important these rituals are to the postmodern believer that they are willing to accommodate by moving the rituals to another location. Some pastors have moved with them, but because life-cycle rituals are designed to be experienced within a faith community, they may lose their "religious" aspect if they are done in the backyard by a justice of the peace. With the increasing rate of divorce, pastors have a specialty of premarital counseling, one that no other human service or legal professional is equipped to provide.

What is a religious ritual? It is a prescribed pattern of act-speech, words that perform action, invoking a divine blessing. Some rituals are considered "sacramental"—for example, communion—which separates them from life-cycle rituals, which mark a "rite of passage" from one phase of faith development onto another. Baptism is both a sacramental and life-cycle ritual. During this rite of passage, worshipers are asked to make a vow to those receiving the ritual and thus, it matters who is worshiping during the ritual. In baptism, worshipers promise to nurture the child's (or adult's) spiritual development. In a wedding ceremony, worshipers promise to support the union of two people. In a funeral, worshipers promise to comfort those who mourn. Because we tend to perform these rituals with an emphasis on the individual(s), the focus has been away from the worshiping community and the spiritual energy that they generate to make the ritual "religious."

Our culture has few rituals to celebrate the life cycle. Even though I am not going to speak about confirmation, because most traditional churches already have an extensive two-year program that is creative and energizes the youth, the act of confirmation is one of the most important life-cycle rituals of the church. We have few indicators that mark the end of childhood and entrance into adulthood. Almost all cultures have some ritual to celebrate this transition. In Western culture, we associate being able to drink alcohol, being able to vote or being responsible to engage in sex as the rite of passage into adulthood. Most of us would probably disagree that being able to drink, vote, or have sex is what launches one into an adult journey of faith. Yet, because religious organizations take a backseat to progress, culture has looked for other indicators of adulthood.

In this chapter, I look at each of the three life-cycle rituals— baptism, weddings, and funerals—that are windows of opportunity to attract the postmodern believer. My central idea is that the postmodern believer must have opportunities to engage in holy interactions and make meaningful relationships with not only other worshipers, but with others who are making similar life transitions, for themselves or for their children. Thus, this chapter is not only an extension of chapter 2, but chapter 3 as well, as engagement in life-cycle rituals is an aspect of invitational and welcoming evangelism. For the church that has designed itself as a contemporary one, those who request life-cycle rituals and make these contacts will also have their perceptions of the church as an "outdated" institution challenged.

BAPTISM

There is an old joke about bats in a belfry and a congregation that discusses how to get rid of them until one insightful individual determines that if they are baptized and confirmed, they will never be seen again. I used to think that joke was funny, but now it stings of postmodern reality. Years ago, when a parent contacted the church about having their child "done," I would visit with them. I still believed that if they liked me and I could convince them that the church was the "happening" place to be, I could hook them to come to church from thereon. This misperception only ended up with a lot of nights out for the pastor. How does a congregation reverse this pattern?

When a parent calls the church for a baptism, our secretary takes the information and then those requesting baptism are invited to attend a worship service to introduce themselves to the pastor, but more importantly, to experience a contemporary worship service and meet other people. If this is the place in which they feel called to raise their children in faith, they are then invited to attend a "parents group" for those who are baptizing their children or who have recently had their children baptized. This cell group is composed of mostly "young" people, some with older children and some who are new to parenthood. When the cell group is more than twelve parents, another group is formed based on another variable that determines them as a subset, such as new parents or single parents.

In the church of yesterday, these groups were often referred to as "mothers groups" but with the changing role of fatherhood in our contemporary culture, we include both parents so as to encourage both parents to be involved with the raising their children in faith. A leader is equipped to set the agenda, and often they have guest speakers who specialize in parenting issues, some who specialize in issues specific to motherhood or fatherhood. The leader also encourages holy interactions among those in the group and encourages them to invite others to this group. The meaning of baptism is addressed, but the focus is on the issues for the parents themselves: the transition into parenthood and the adjustments that are often made. These transitions are met with ease when they have a group of other new parents who offer support.

The traditional meaning of baptism is preserved through these groups. Before we instituted the groups, we found that what most postmodern believers were looking for when they contacted the church was a blessing, not a baptism. We had to struggle with whether or not we might offer a blessing for those who have no intention of returning to raise their child in the Christian faith. Because we have made every effort not to "sell out" for the mere purpose of attracting the postmodern believer, we shifted not our theology of baptism but the way in which we prepared the believer to receive baptism. Our experience has been that we "lose" very few postmodern believers who bring their child to be baptized.

We understand that baptism is also an act of signing up for our Christian education program, and we offer this program beginning at age two. Every so often, we meet a parent who says that they do not want to choose the child's religion for them. But we respond, "If you do not raise your child in a faith community, you have already chosen for them." Thus, the group also focuses on raising children in the Christian education program, and many in the group will participate as leaders in that program. Because some postmodern believers are anxious about allowing adults whom they do not know to take care of their children, we make every effort to ensure their safety.

Creating a safe environment is not only avoiding an insurance liability, but it should be an intentional and well-thought-out policy. It should be something that is talked about openly, under the operative assumption that the more people who are part of the discussion, the stricter the policies that will be implemented and the more people who will know that such policies are in effect. In our church, we do not change diapers, but we give a parent a buzzer, the same technology that many restaurants use when one is waiting for a table. If the child has to be changed, the parent is buzzed, and he or she leaves the sanctuary (most of us know where they are going) to attend to their child. This device also assures a worried parent that if they are needed, they will be immediately notified. We also have a nurse, not teenagers, taking care of babies. Most of the current models of policy making for safe environments suggest that one adult is never alone with a child, but two adults are in the same classroom at any one time. Because churches should create safe environments, not only in their Sunday school rooms but in their congregational functioning, we extend these policies throughout the church.

Baptism is a commitment to raise one's child in the church's Christian education program. But when a congregation responds to the ritual of baptism by promising to provide an environment that is conducive to learning, it must also be willing to provide enough money in this area for contemporary technology, for example, DVDs, music, or PowerPoint. Classrooms should be painted bright contemporary colors (and not the pale yellow of the 1960s). Adults with or without children in the program should be included in the program by their visiting the Sunday school classroom to share something about their faith or their daily living. These visits are also an opportunity for holy interactions. Under supervision, there should be opportunities for adults in the church to interact with children in meaningful ways. Intergenerational interactions are another way that we are unique from other social organizations.

WEDDINGS

Contemporary cultural trends do not encourage couples to be married. Because it is considered socially acceptable to live together and even have children together, and given the high divorce rate, fewer couples are getting married than a generation ago. Even fewer are seeking out weddings within the church. Some complain this is because it is too expensive these days to get married within a church. Others "just want to get married and don't want to have to jump through all the hoops" of classes to prepare for marriage or meeting with the pastor. With the availability of the justice of the peace, this enables many couples to bypass premarital counseling.

Premarital counseling is not only a specialty, but because it is unique to the church, pastors should receive training for it in seminary. Too often, the focus is on the wedding service itself and not on the impending marriage. The dress colors of the bridesmaids, the dinner at the reception, and whether or not the photographer is allowed to take pictures in the sanctuary become the topic of conversation, rather than how the couple manages conflict, supports each other during times of crisis, and affirms one another's relational qualities. I routinely ask about abuse and tell the couple that "If I don't ask, no one else will." Having been married myself for twenty-six years, I believe that couples need to have a plan of action for, not if, but when they go through struggles. That plan of action needs to be in place before the problems arise. If the couple waits until after the wedding, they will not be in the mood to construct such a plan.

For those couples getting married for a second time or more, premarital counseling is essential to identify the problems that arose in the first marriage, in order to prevent them from being repeated. We develop relational skills in our family of origin. We tend to choose a spouse based on these dynamics, consciously or unconsciously. When we raise the couple's awareness of these dynamics, they are able to make better decisions about the ways in which they relate and to control those patterns of relating that tend to cause pain and frustration.

We also offer what we call a "wedding seminar," which functions similar to the parents group. Wedding seminar is an opportunity for several couples who are planning a wedding to get together and discuss relationship issues. The leader uses a curriculum designed to cover an array of pertinent issues and to educate and encourage sharing joys and struggles to facilitate holy interactions. Topics range from fair arguing, anger management, and generational cycles of abuse, in addition to how to manage finances, balance recreation and work time, and housekeeping tasks. There is an emphasis on the spiritual, emotional, and practical aspects of a marriage.

FUNERALS

All cultures have rituals to bury their dead. During emotionally charged times such as the death of a loved one, most people want the ritual performed the way that it has been preformed in their culture.

Such a ritual helps the mourner through the grieving process, provides a setting to express sadness, and equips others to be a source of support and strength. Whereas baptisms and weddings are associated with feelings of joy and celebration, funerals are usually times of sorrow, anger, and emptiness. Outside of wakes, memorials, and funerals, our society has few other ways of grieving our dead. If organized religion is to survive in any form, it will be at least for the purpose of burying our loved ones with the hope of an afterlife.

When the modern worshiper experiences the loss of a loved one, they turn to their church family for this comfort. They have already invested energy into making these holy connections and so that comfort is easily available. But the postmodern believer may have almost no association with a congregation after the death of a loved one. They make arrangements through a funeral director, who contacts a local pastor to do the service, and then the local pastor contacts the family. Often the family has no previous relationship with the pastor, so the pastor may ask questions about the loved one in order to prepare for leading the funeral service. The church is not viewed as a source of comfort, but the place of employment for the pastor who "did" the service for them. While they may like the pastor and have felt comforted by the pastor, it is unlikely that this will be a window of opportunity to engage them.

In a contemporary congregation, grief is viewed as an ongoing process from the immediate loss through all the ways that that loss impacts a person's life. We offer a support group for those who have experienced a loss, and this group is led by a disciple who is trained in grief counseling. The group is not limited to the loss that is experienced at the time of death, but includes the loss of relationships through empty nest, divorce, or the loss of any other significant relationship; the loss of a body function through disease, illness or accident; the loss of a pet, and more. The experience of one loss tends to revive all the previous losses experienced, and so we see this group as an opportunity to learn coping skills to deal with the experience of loss in general. Some enter our loss group having lost a family pet and then reveal that they are also grieving a more tragic loss, such as the loss of a child.

Our Maundy Thursday worship service recognizes that the funeral does not end the process of grieving, but begins it. We send out invitations to all those in our community who suffered a loss over the past year. During a candle lighting ceremony, we invite everyone to come forward to the chancel and sign our remembrance book. The worship leader begins the ceremony with suggestions of what might be written in the book. Most people write a message such as "we miss you" or "we love you." While that is going on at the chancel, people in the pews are instructed to pray for those who are signing. It is one of the most intimate moments in the life of the congregation. We also encourage everyone to attend, especially those who have not experienced a recent loss in order to serve as the instruments for God's comfort and healing. On Easter morning, the names of the saints are read from the pulpit as our affirmation of faith that they are with Jesus in heaven.

A healthy contemporary congregation nurtures the free expression of emotions. In most other social organizations, we hide our feelings for fear of being judged. Our culture enables people to repress their feelings with the use of drugs and alcohol, shopping and buying nonessential items, and multitasking to remain in a busy state. We have few opportunities in our culture to remain still and allow our emotions to come to the surface. Spiritual growth is dependent upon emotional expression. People are looking for a place where it is considered acceptable to be in touch with their feelings. Organized religion tends to resist being that social organization for people because creating that kind of an environment is a risk. But it is a risk worth taking.

Our children closely observe the reactions of the adults in the congregation during a time of loss. They learn what is acceptable based on these observations. They take note of whether or not adults cry when they hear sad news or if they "keep a stiff upper lip." If they see their parents return home to cry after a worship service, they may get the message that crying is not something that is done in community, but in the privacy of one's own home. When holy interactions are nurtured within a congregation, children learn that church is the place to express these feelings and, if they do so, there will be others available to them for strength, courage, and support. After a good cry with everyone else in a congregation, people find that they feel better. Instead of pushing these feelings down so that they have the potential to be destructive, contemporary congregations encourage the free expression of emotions.

seven | denominationalism

I grew up attending Pleasant St. Congregational Church in Arlington, Massachusetts. When I went to seminary, I was asked, "What denomination are you?" and I answered, "Congregational." That answer often invoked the follow-up question, "Are you UCC.?" but I had not heard of the United Church of Christ. So I called up my father and asked if we were members of the United Church of Christ. He said, "I think that was the group we voted to join years ago." Our congregation had voted to join the denomination, but we marginally identified ourselves with the denomination. After some discernment, and acclimating myself to the functioning of the denomination, I chose to be ordained in the United Church of Christ because of its focus on Jesus and its history of social justice advocacy and action.

The modern worshiper participates in the life of the local church and develops a sense of belonging to its denomination. They are loyal to their denomination, and when they retire to another community, they are likely to seek out a church affiliated with that denomination. To some extent, the modern worshiper is more loyal to their denomination and less to the local church, especially for those modern worshipers whose personal life is in transition. For example, they may not have set foot in a local church for some time and may still claim that they are Methodist. The modern worshiper is often unaware of the differences between one denomination and another. Their religious identity is with their own denomination not based on policy, theology, or practice, but based on loyalty.

More recently, however, the modern worshiper has become ambivalent toward their denomination, especially denominations experiencing congregational depression. The denomination itself becomes one more target for the congregation to blame its woes upon. This has strained the relationship between the local church and the denomination. Further, when a denomination attempts to take a stance on an issue of social justice and the local church disagrees with that stance, the local church's response is often to threaten its voluntary association with the denomination (which can also be said for churches associated with a denomination that functions as a covenantal association).

The postmodern believer, now moving into realm of organized religion, looks toward the denomination as another place to gather with other newly evangelizing believers and is therefore also supportive of the denomination in its function as the umbrella organization. Having had a positive experience with the local congregation, they are interested in the workings of this umbrella organization and are eager to participate in organized religion at another level. The postmodern believer views denominational affiliation as another way to invest energy into something that yields spiritual energy in return (karmic balance).

Contrary to the postmodern prophecy that warns of "postdenominationalism," I foresee denominationalism as an important aspect of congregational functioning in the contemporary congregation. In order to survive, denominationalism needs to be redesigned to be more aligned with postmodern culture. Like the congregation, the denomination continues to function as a reflection of modern culture, and yet postmodern culture no longer is interested in what it has to say. The agenda passed at denominational conventions rarely makes it to the media.

Karmic balance, the mutual exchange of energy between two systems, must function between the local congregation and the denomination to sustain a healthy relationship where one energizes the other. But because the denomination serves as the umbrella organization, it is the denomination's responsibility to energize the congregation when it becomes depressed (not the other way around). To discuss the five functions of the contemporary denomination, I will use the acronym SERVE, which stands for the active verbs 1) supporting clergy, 2) encouraging competition, 3) resisting dualism, 4) visualizing identity, and 5) evolving synergy.

SUPPORTING CLERGY

Early on in my ministry, I was blessed with two wise sages who each shared with me their experience of being a parish minister as they were celebrating their retirement. The first one said that his only regret about being a parish minister was that he spent too much time in the office at the neglect of his family and, if he could do it all again, he would have made more time for his children growing up. His words echo within me whenever I think about "doing one more thing" before I go home. I will literally drop everything on the floor (my office is always a mess!) and close the door and remind myself that "it will be there tomorrow." In the profession of the ministry, there is no built-in signal that alerts us that we are finished for the day. Knowing when to set that boundary is important (especially so that pastors do not over-function for the congregation).

The second sage spoke of "the bone-crushing loneliness" of being a parish minister. I can still feel the sadness with which he spoke about what is it like to be in a profession where we work solo rather than with colleagues. Most other professions practice side by side with those performing similar functions. Even though some churches have multiple pastors, there is usually one senior pastor. The associate pastors may be colleagues, but the senior pastor is responsible for what happens and thus functions with more authority and power. Because pastors are either placed or move to serve their next church, there are few opportunities to make friends with people socially, especially given that every friend may be a potential parishioner.

One of the most important contemporary functions of denominationalism will be the support of clergy, nurturing their relationships between each other and holding them to accountability. Programs for clergy tend to focus on training and continuing education as well as networking resources among the churches. There are fewer opportunities just to hang together and to openly share the joys and struggles of the parish ministry and its day-to-day functioning. Until we foster holy interactions among clergy, we will struggle to nurture this level of intimacy among parishioners in our churches. When the denomination is able to encourage emotional connection among clergy, it will experience the benefit of encouraging its congregations to take similar risks.

Events such as luncheons are often not considered part of one's job and so these gatherings are perceived as an "extra" task when the pastor has enough time to fit another activity into their already busy schedule. The programs themselves offer professional development, but far less frequently avenues for spiritual growth. Pastors are often running to one event from another and such constant movement, when not balanced with quiet times beside still waters, will use up pastor's energy and may cause depression. Depressed clergy tend to underfunction, and underfunctioning pastors tend to energize the congregation to target the pastor for criticism.

"All because I didn't do lunch?" Pastors need emotional support from their colleagues. Without this support, their spiritual energy will wane and their spiritual connection with God will suffer. Clergy function with a mentality that says, "If I am not helping someone else at the moment I am not doing my job." We tend to feel guilty when it comes to taking time for ourselves and our spirituality. If personal spirituality is manifested as congregational vitality, as I am proposing throughout this book, then pastors must take the lead in spiritual self-care. Only when clergy self-care becomes more of a priority in denominations will we have healthier congregations. Emotionally healthy clergy mentor emotionally healthy congregations.

Historically, it has been considered acceptable for a pastor to befriend a parishioner. The single male pastor is often the pawn among matchmakers within the congregation who wish to work their magic by linking him up with a single woman. In every other profession, "dual relationships," that is, relationships which begin as professional and transport into personal, are a violation of ethical conduct. Parishioners need a pastor, not another friend. Those who engage in sexual acting-out have crossed this boundary line and therefore they are not in a position to be able to objectively understand the unequal distribution of power between themselves and this other person. Pastors who engage in such acting-out behavior usually suffer from underlying depression and need support before their judgment is impaired to see this relationship as "appropriate."

The design of healthy denominational support of clergy should focus on prevention rather than secondary intervention such as treatment for acting-out behavior or punishment for illegal actions. The denomination should design safeguards for pastors who reach a point when they are no longer emotionally healthy. The denomination itself, its officials, and those who are responsible for providing support should be skilled in prevention strategies in order to stop an out-of-control pastor from spiraling downward. After all, when the incident reaches the press, it is the denomination's reputation on the defensive. In this day and age, most postmodern believers are already suspicious of clergy and umbrella organizations that enable clergy sexual abuse. By implementing policies and programs of prevention, acting-out among clergy will be less likely.

When conflict arises between the pastor and the congregation, it is a conflict of interests for denominational officials to come to "help." Denominational officials are paid by the congregation and their loyalty is with the congregation. When they tell the pastor that they will come and offer support, the subtext is "support of the congregation," but the pastor expects that the denomination will support the pastor. Denominational officials, however, are more likely to "side" with those who pay their salaries. Pastors often leave the meeting feeling betrayed, alone, and wrong. The pastor becomes more depressed and more the target of the congregation's negative energy. Instead of helping, the denomination may actually enable the conflict to continue.

Instead of the preceding scenario, the denomination and the clergy together should hire a mediator who is trained in dispute resolution. A mediator would have no prior relationship with either the pastor or the congregation and have no emotional investment in the outcome. Mediators are particularly skilled at resolving conflict by identifying the positive aspects of the pastor's relationship with the congregation and capitalizing on that, as well as helping both the pastor and the congregation to develop empathy to understand the other's positions. Mediators can lend insight into the dynamics of the pastor-parish relationship and seek to preserve that relationship.

Denominational officials often refer to themselves as "the pastor to the pastors." But this self-perception is also unrealistic. Seasoned pastors learn early on not to share intimate details of their struggles with those in positions of authority who will make decisions and determine their next placement. Most denominations function under the policy of placement, even if, as in the United Church of Christ, pastors are selected by being called by a specific congregation. Denominational officials orchestrate the placement process by offering "support" to the congregation, and that involvement alone is cause for most pastors to be suspicious about this dual function.

I suggest that the contemporary pastor and denomination hire both an outside consultant to mediate conflict as well as a "pastor to the pastors." These would be two separate positions. A pastor to the pastors and a mediator would be required to keep the confidentiality of the pastor, which would increase the likelihood that the pastor would feel comfortable sharing their emotional and spiritual life. Without this opportunity, pastors feel they have no one to talk to and may overburden family members and friends with their personal and professional struggles. Family members and friends, who by nature of their relationship are not objective, do not know how to help and they themselves become overwhelmed because they want to help. In order to fund both of these positions, pastors would not give financially to their church's budgets (pastors are often the biggest contributors to their stewardship programs to set the model) but to someone who manages this money independent of both the congregation and the denomination.

Years ago, I suggested that groups of pastors and their families worship together on Sunday evenings. I admit, I do not feel I fully worship as a liturgical artist. I am still responsible for what is happening in worship and I cannot zone out if I feel like doing so. A denomination that worshiped together on a weekly basis would experience holy interactions. Just as parishioners experience support from one another, as in "I could not have pulled myself through without the support of my church," pastors would be able to provide support for one another. A parallel process would be set in place where pastors could also assess what it is like to be a parishioner and how it feels to participate in worship using different worship styles. Then, pastors may be more willing to introduce change.

The response I received to this idea of weekly worship as a faith community of clergy and their families was that clergy are supposed to worship within their own faith community and that they are too busy to have another night out. The "busy" response is the same one that I hear when I run into a parishioner I have not seen for awhile. I understand that in some places in America, worshiping together would be very time-consuming, given the distance one has to travel to the home of the denomination, but in New England, most clergy do not have to drive more than an hour to be at another church in their denomination. I encourage clergy to travel an hour to attend church just like I encourage parishioners to drive an hour from their neighborhood. The idea of "the neighborhood church" is eroding as more and more people make a long drive to a church, especially those who are committed to multiculturalism. Clergy could model this movement outside of their neighborhood to produce holy interactions.

ENCOURAGING COMPETITION

Almost every year for the past eight years, I have run the Boston Marathon. Several years ago a reporter for the *Boston Globe* interviewed me and asked about my strategy to make it up Heartbreak Hill (a grueling incline between miles 17 and 21) and I responded, "I intend to pray." (The interview appeared in the *Boston Globe* in April 2000 and was titled, "She'll Seek Help from Above on Heartbreak Hill.") As one runs up the hill, other runners are crunched over in agony on the grass, some requiring medical attention for dehydration, others are just out of energy and unable to go any further. I also said in the article that running is not about moving one's legs back and forth but about endurance: running is a metaphor for life that Jesus has taught me—to keep moving forward through the pain and stay focused on him.

I am never going to win the Boston Marathon, but that doesn't matter; what matters is that I train and run as if there is a slight possibility that I might just win it. Such faith may be outside the realm of rationality, but I believe that "with God all things are possible." Relationships, by nature, have a competitive aspect within them: perhaps competition brings out the best of who we are and our potential for transformation. As Paul says in 1 Corinthians, "Do you not know that in a race the runners all compete, but only one receives the prize? Run in such a way that you may win it" (9:24). We need to encourage competition among the local congregations, among denominations, that we may help motivate and move each other to run in order to win.

The Christian church is currently trekking up Heartbreak Hill. What will distinguish the churches that make it to the top and survive this time of trial will be the character of endurance to tolerate fear, change, fear of change, discomfort, discouragement, frustration, anger, and so on, and the trust that these feelings are part of the process when an organization is making a high-impact change in its attempt to get to the top of the mountain and see God's vision on the horizon. Those congregations with upward momentum will pray for the casualties of postmodern culture who will close because of dehydration of finances and lack of energy. The mainstream Protestant church has come so far, running the good race in its history and tradition, that it pains me to see some suffer the sting of death and the agony of defeat.

Those churches that are running past us with vigor and enthusiasm are those churches running as a relay team who will pass the baton to another kind of church, that is, evangelical to postevangelical. Mainline Protestantism cannot expect to run as fast. In the evangelical movement, this vision emphasized numerically large megachurches, with loud booming rock music and charismatic preaching from a good-looking male pastor. People were brought into the movement through persuasive techniques that targeted certain homogenous groups of people (often young and affluent). These churches' mission is to transform secular space into sacred space, so they hold church in a bar or a nightclub. The movement is toward a numerically large, leaderless, non-denominational group that is not tied down by a building.[1]

I am overwhelmed by the numbers bragged about by church growth specialists associated with the postevangelical movement. They envision that a contemporary design should focus on multiplication, or what they refer to as "reproducing DNA." This means to take a congregation of five hundred in worship attendance and turn it into a congregation of five thousand. With average attendance in mainline Protestant churches less than one hundred, our exponential growth will warrant a different set of strategies, more appropriate for the turtle in this race. I am not a very fast runner, but I am consistent and make it to the finish line.

Even if we are running the race together, we can compete with one another. Local churches within the same denomination may compete with each other but should be seen as "one team." Even those on the same team on the soccer field will compete with one another to bring out the best in one another. I suggest that the level of what constitutes a "team" should be the denomination and not the local church, because then it would see the denomination itself as a competitor. The denominational teams are composed of their own local churches and therefore the denomination itself would have an investment in seeing that the local church wins by attracting the postmodern believer, and sister churches would help each other.

We all want to be part of a winning team. If the Red Sox and the Yankees were to no longer keep score of the game, they would undoubtedly have fewer fans. People get caught up in the energy that is generated by winning. Most of us would rather attend the celebration of the political candidate who wins the campaign than mope around at the headquarters of the loser. When we invite the postmodern believer to the loser's headquarters, why would they want to come? It's a downer. No one wants to be around a group of people whose spiritual energy has been depleted, drained, and downgraded. The local denomination that projects the image of winning the race will inspire their local churches, and that energy will produce numerical growth. (Numerical growth is a natural byproduct of spiritual growth.)

In the present state of denominational depression, officials inadvertently enable too much competition among the local churches themselves, which divides rather than unites as a team. The large churches are often considered to be the churches served by the more competent pastors. Because we have all bought into this myth, pastors who are the most competent are drawn to the numerically larger churches (which also tend to pay better), and the less competent, or may I say the less experienced, pastors tend to go to the numerically smaller churches. But because the numerically smaller churches are more likely to be depressed than the larger churches, they need more help, and thus seasoned pastors may have the experience to help then. Also, the larger churches tend to be good at lay empowerment and so may be better served by less experienced pastors, who may need more time and energy to develop their pastoral identity.

Team members should also play fairly. When there are not enough postmodern believers interested in organized religion, what is happening is that local congregations are stealing modern worshipers from one another. The idea should not be to attract modern worshipers, but postmodern believers (those who are not affiliated with organized religion). Stealing modern worshipers, one by one, from a sister church that is struggling to survive is a short-term strategy: eventually, the pool of resources will run dry.

Sheep stealing also enables the modern worshiper to sustain dysfunctional patterns of relating. The modern worshiper who is angry toward the pastor storms out and begins attending the church down the street. This church welcomes the modern worshiper with open arms because the harvest is plentiful and the laborers are few. The modern worshiper exclaims, "This is such a great church because they were so welcoming to me!" and splits the two sister churches into the good one and the bad one. The good one is the new church and the bad one is the one that keeps the pastor with whom they are angry. Like the experience of immigrants who idealize America and devalue the place of their birth, eventually the tides turn the other way, and the modern worshiper finds themselves in the same situation as before, but now they are angry at the pastor of their new church. The risk of sheep stealing hooks pastors and congregation to avoid change, which is often what makes a modern worshiper angry.

As a team competing with other denominations, the denomination itself will be seen as more of a coach than an authority figure. The congregations will look toward the denomination to develop a plan of action and then get out into the field with sister churches and build one another up. Rather than each congregation playing the numbers game as a measure of "success," we will emphasis spiritual development and practices and seek to produce karmic balance by energizing each other.

RESISTING DUALISM

Pilgrims ventured to this land in order to secure religious freedom for themselves and for their children. But an interesting dynamic unfolded. Feeling marginalized to produce change in the face of the dominant power of the Church of England, they became "separatists." When they crossed over the Atlantic and became the dominant group themselves, they hoarded power just as the dominant group had done to them. Any group that the early Protestors deemed as inferior to their status as the dominant group were either banished to Rhode Island, as were the Baptists, or burned on the stake like the Salem witches. Thus America embodied a sociological phenomenon known as "dualism" or, briefly stated, a dynamic of "us against them." When we compete with one another, there is a natural tendency to use dualism as a mode of functioning.

This tendency polarizes the dominant and marginalized groups. The dominant group is the group with power and tries to assert that power over the marginalized group. The autonomous nature of congregational policy instills in their ethos a resistance against the dominant group based on this history. Instead the relationship between the denomination and the local congregation should be one of karmic balance; that is, energy flows between the two systems in a mutually supportive relationship. When the denomination attempts to take a stance on an issue, the local congregation often perceives this surge of power as "the denomination telling us what to do." Most congregations seek to function as independent, autonomous organizations loosely associated with their denominations.

I remember the one time I said, "But our denomination, the United Church of Christ, has voted that we should do it!" It was the closest I have come to being spit out of the church. While it is important for the denomination to take a stance on issues of social justice, that stance can carry the implication that the denomination is imposing its authority upon the congregation. Yet the denomination itself is comprised of voting representatives from each of the congregations and essentially, beyond officials, constitutes the denomination. Since the United Church of Christ took its stance on supporting legislation for gay and lesbian persons to be legally married, some, though few, congregations perceived this as the Mother Church of England, once again, trying to control them, and they protested by withdrawing.

Denominationalism needs to move itself out of the radar of being the "authority figure" to be resisted by the local church. Every year at annual meeting someone in our church asks about the money that we pay to support the denomination and what we get for it in return. What they are questioning is the issue of karmic balance, which, in a consumer-driven society, asks, "Are we getting what we pay for?" The relationship between the denomination and the local church must be of mutual benefit and exchange of energy. When the visibility of denominational officials, programs, and social justice efforts is low, the denomination runs the risk of a mass rebellion in our postmodern culture. While the modern worshiper in the modern culture used to approach denominationalism as "Ask not what your denomination does for you, but what you can do for your denomination," the modern worshiper in postmodern culture asks, "What does the denomination do for us?"

The Christian church has historically and traditionally approached religion as dualistic: heaven and earth, sacred and secular, good people and bad people, saints and sinners, those who are saved and those who are not. The contemporary congregation will move away from dualism. As Martin Luther inspired the reformation by seeing the saint and the sinner existing within each one of us, to reconcile the present-day dualism of either-or, so will the contemporary congregation move away from the dynamic of "splitting." The movement away from dualistic thinking is toward a tolerance for ambiguity, the gray area where the boundary between the categories is seen on a continuum on which we can plot our current location, but which position is subject to change. Heaven is no longer viewed as "above the clouds" in some remote part of the universe, but transparent upon the earth and only viewable under certain conditions.

Multiculturalism, which seeks to break down the boundary line between the dominant and marginalized, offers a new paradigm to dualism. James Thwaites advocates for a return to Hebrew worldview, predualism, to design contemporary congregations.[2] This may be a compelling area of research for further study. Suffice it is to say here that dualism may foster competition, but its ramifications can be destructive and should be resisted. We can identify who we are with images; we do not need to define who we are by scapegoating another to define who we are not. This pattern of identification has failed to produce any substance for visualizing our religious identity. We need fresh images to speak of who we are as a religious organization, not based on who we are not, for example, conservative or liberal, but based on our perceptions of who we are as the body of Christ.

VISUALIZING IDENTITY

As a denomination we do not know who we are. In the United Church of Christ this may be partly due to the recent merger (1959) of four distinct denominations into one. Each of those denominations had an established identity, but together they have yet to embrace a common identity. This lack of identity trickles down to the local congregation, who retains their previous identity, at least in name, for example, "The First Congregational Church." If the denomination does not take seriously this current crisis to visualize its identity, I would suspect that we will see more and more churches returning to traditional images of their identity as defined by their past denomination. The anxiety of the wilderness is just too much for most people, especially if there is no leader who thinks they know the way out.

The current dialogue in the Massachusetts conference focuses on the notion of "covenant" among the churches as a way to build cohesion and foster team unity. The problem is that without an identity there is nothing to covenant about. Because we celebrate "diversity in unity," we have yet to identify a unifying principle that in the midst of diversity we can all agree upon as the glue that keeps us together. We will need to decide whether or not that unifying principle is faith based or simply the polity under which we function, or both. What it should not convey is something negative about another denomination, suggesting, for instance, that another faith or denomination is exclusive of gay and lesbian persons, as if our denomination has fully embraced the idea. When we define who we are, that definition should reflect current reality, not a prophecy of who we hope to become.

Many denominations are attempting to form an identity based on "a visioning process." This process buys the denomination a little more time to discern "who it is" but has yet to produce much substance. When someone speaks to me about "a vision" for the future of a denomination, I want to know what that vision looks like in practical terms, in religious and spiritual practice, how it will effect what I do as pastor of a congregation, and what the disciples of Jesus will be called to do in their service to the community. I want that identity to say something about the relationship between the local church and the denomination. Too much emphasis has been misplaced on waiting for a miraculous revelation of a vision instead of delving into the contemporizing process and witnessing to that vision unfolding before us.

Identity is key to contemporizing the denomination because it also encourages and sustain loyalty. If the modern worshiper is already loyal and feels a sense of belonging to the denomination, they will access energy in order to sustain that relationship. The postmodern believer will witness this loyalty and will follow their lead as long as the denomination is willing to make the needed changes to be congruent with contemporary culture.

Identity is also related to the issue of visibility. Denominations are often hidden from view, not only with respect to their cultural environment but among the local churches themselves. Denominational officials should, at least annually, come to the local congregation and be among the team of worship leaders. If parishioners do not hear what is happening in the denomination from the officials themselves, then they will not be motivated to fund what is happening and will complain about any money that is sent to the denomination. Lack of visibility has contributed to this unequal karmic balance of the denominations being some huge entity to which the local congregation gives money and receives little or nothing in return.

Identity is formed based on a series of images. Paul invoked imagery to speak of the local congregation. He spoke of the church as brothers and sisters in Christ and as the body of Christ with members who are each gifted by the Spirit to fulfill different functions. The metaphor of the "body" has been particularly relevant to people in postmodern culture, who spend time at a health club in the morning getting in shape. As a friend of mine recently commented, "Whenever I go to church, I have to drag myself there. But after I am there and when I leave, I feel good and I am glad that I went. I feel the same way about going to a health club in the morning." Our fresh images may emphasis our physical, spiritual, and emotional health because congregations are in a unique position to be able to develop all three: an all-inclusive social organization.

Developing a denominational identity will also encourage ecumenism. When we know who we are as a denomination, we will be less threatened to interact with others. Identity formation will give us the freedom to be curious about global religions and what other religious practices may be tweaked to be relevant to Christian practice. In our depressed state, we worry that encouraging this curiosity will result in losing adherents. Ecumenical dialogue, however, may be key to peace-keeping efforts with our international relations.

C. Kirk Hadaway and David Roozen, in *Rerouting the Protestant Mainstream,* argue that denominations should be replaced with "movements."[3] If the local congregation is imaged as the stream that flows to social justice, the denomination should be the source of that flow. It should create energy and enthusiasm for the contemporary congregation. Movement provides an image of change rather than status quo, or flowing rather than stagnancy, or accessing energy rather than its suppression. I am not too concerned about what we will call this umbrella organization, but it should be a culmination of contemporary images that genuinely reflects who we are and to whom we belong.

EVOKING SYNERGY

When spiritual energy comes together en mass, it is known as "synergy." It is often said that what we cannot do alone, we can do together. In a culture where "bigger is better," the postmodern believer will perceive the small church as having "less" to offer than the larger church, especially in terms of variety of ways to get involved. The small church will struggle more to attract the postmodern believer for this reason. Thus the future of the small church may be in its identification with the larger denomination and its willingness to share resources with sister congregations.

I foresee denominationalism functioning in the future as a point of mediation in church merging. We have so many small churches duplicating their own efforts; yet, if they came together and shared their common resources, such as a pastor, they would have money to engage in contemporizing their congregation. I think it is fairly obvious that churches will not merge on their own: they will need denominational officials to come in and encourage them and then equip them with what is involved to take on this project. This is an example of how the denomination may function as coach.

I am simply amazed that the small church would rather die than merge. I understand that they have a relationship with the setting, but it is time to strengthen parishioners' relationships with Jesus rather than the building that they believe Jesus dwells in. It is like when a young child sees me in a grocery store and is in awe that the church "lets me out" of the building. When the denomination encourages local churches to engage in spiritual practices outside of the local church, such as coming together for worship as a combination of congregations (not just clergy), they will begin to realize that Jesus can be found in other church buildings. This would also free up some of our church buildings for either renovation and curb appeal or to house a church plant looking for a new home.

Merging may also be a way to access spiritual energy. As two congregations come together, they re-energize one another through developing this new relationship. Holy interactions bring out conversations about faith, and, when two gather together, they may bring out the best in each other. When we enter into the world of another and see the world the way they do, we are in a position to be able to offer assistance. I see church merging as a way to do this because when two churches enter into that relationship, they each have an investment to understand the other in order to accept and encourage change.

The large churches that are both contemporary and healthy (three variables not necessarily present all together, but likely) might "adopt" a smaller congregation. They would do all the congregational functioning—for example, worship, evangelism, social justice—for the small church for one year or until attendance in worship reached 150. The smaller congregation would have to be flexible and might have to adjust the traditional time of their worship service, but the benefits would far outweigh the minor sacrifices that would need to be made. This way, the members of the small congregation could continue to worship in their own sanctuary and be part of a movement toward spiritual and numerical growth. All the larger church would do is share its strategies for attracting the postmodern believer, which emphasizes spiritual growth as a precursor to numerical growth.

In the contemporary design, the denomination will be responsible for "evolving" synergy. This means that when the local congregation is depressed and does not know how to alleviate its depression, the denomination will take an active role in providing avenues for the congregation to re-energize itself. Thus, the energy will evolve from the denomination, both from officials as well as from sister congregations. When the denomination supports clergy, encourages competition, resists dualism, and visuals identity, this energy will flow to the local congregations as an ever-flowing stream.

c o n c l u s i o n

Three days before this manuscript was due at The Pilgrim Press, I received a telephone call to inform me that a thirty-nine-year-old parishioner was found dead in her home. I had taken the last two weeks as vacation away at my home in Maine to finish the book, and on this one Sunday morning, an hour before worship, I said, "I am sorry I am not there. I feel like I should have been there this morning for worship." I had even debated getting in my car and running to the rescue. The disciple paused and replied, "We are sorry too that you are not here but you have taught us how to be there for each other and we will get through this without your physically being with us. We know that you are with us in spirit." I still struggle to break out of the traditional mode of functioning that insists the pastor is the sole instrument of comfort and reconciliation. The church no longer revolves around everything I do, and this has made room for the work of the Holy Spirit.

I feel more valued as the pastor and liturgical artist of a contemporary congregation, even though I do fewer traditional aspects of ministry. Designing and serving a contemporary congregation has given me more time to find out who I am in relation to God and discern my own gifts for future ministry. I feel more spiritually connected to God in everything I do, personally and professionally.

Ecclesiastes boldly claims that "there is nothing new under the sun." In each phase of the church's historical development, it interacted with culture to form its traditions. It is that tradition itself that has been resurrected in this book in order to heal the present crisis of congregational depression. In essence, the strategy presented here has only revived an old congregational tradition. As culture influences the church, the church, in turn, is allowed to influence culture through forms of social justice. Churches who take the alternative approach, that is, to judge or condemn culture, will be resisted in their efforts to exert "redemptive influence."

This approach requires an ongoing commitment to change. For just at the point in which the church aligns itself with contemporary culture, be it modern, postmodern or post-postmodern, culture will continue to progress forward. When the church eventually catches up, it will find that in the race forward, it might even be able to function as a leader or forerunner of society. This will be evident when the church returns to its status of promoting socially just patterns of relating within its functioning to serve as a model for other social organizations to emulate. When congregations become multicultural, this will be a good indication that it is in the position of forerunner.

The religious practices presented in this book will eventually become as outdated as their predecessors. What will continue about the contemporary congregation and its relation to a postmodern environment is ongoing change itself. Some speak of the church as traditional, contemporary, transformational, and so forth, but a more forward thinking designation would be "transitional." The church is in a constant state of flux, moving from one point to another, a pilgrimage to the promised land, never quite arriving, but spiritually growing along the way.

Transition is not a strange concept for the church. Every congregation finds itself in the midst of some sort of transition. It may be as simple as the transition of people rotating on and off various boards and committees. It could be the transition that occurs when a once vital congregation loses momentum and members. But I want to offer a new definition of the transitional congregation—a church in transition to a positive, future-embracing vision that says, "We have not yet experienced this congregation's greatest ministry. Let us bless what God has done among us and add the ministry we believe will touch another circle of people."[1]

Realigning itself with culture will produce change, and that change uses the principle of karmic balance, which will produce spiritual growth, the basis for attracting the postmodern generation. Not every church will bear the fruits of this harvest. The choice is whether we design new congregations within the sacred place of traditional buildings or we plant new church starts. This book witnesses to the willingness and ability of the traditional congregation to design itself as contemporary.

n o t e s

PREFACE

1. Stephen C. Compton, *Rekindling the Mainline: New Life though New Churches* (Bethesda, Md.: Alban Institute, 2003).

2. Michael Jinkins, *The Church Faces Death: Ecclesiology in a Post-Modern Context* (New York: Oxford University Press, 1999), 12.

INTRODUCTION

1. In the Unites States, it is estimated that 20 percent of all Americans are affiliated with organized religion. We might also speculate that that estimate represents a large portion of recent immigrants who preserve their culture through organized religion. For a discussion on statistics, see George Barna, *Turn-Around Churches: How to Overcome Barriers to Growth and Bring New Life to an Established Church* (Ventura, Calif.: Regal Books, 1993).

2. The glory days were filled with such a good feeling that several parishioners wanted to ensure their beloved church would continue to serve the next generation and left a legacy of money to the church preserved as an endowment. They wanted to make sure that their great grandchildren would have a place to worship God and to receive the same benefits of being part of a faith community as they had received. It is ironic, and quite sad, that what most endowments sustain today is a slow death. Without an endowment, a dying church would be out of its misery and not confronted by such difficult and painful issues.

3. John B. Cobb Jr., *Reclaiming the Church: Where the Mainline Church Went Wrong and What to Do about It* (Louisville: Westminster John Knox Press, 1997), 43.

4. See Thomas G. Bandy, *Moving Off the Map: A Field Guide to Changing the Congregation* (Nashville: Abingdon Press, 1998).

CHAPTER 1

1. Rick Warren, *The Purpose-Driven Church: Growth without Compromising Your Message & Mission* (Grand Rapids: Zondervan, 1995), 62.

CHAPTER 3

1. Thomas G. Bandy. *Moving Off the Map: A Field Guide to Changing the Congregation* (Nashville: Abingdon Press, 1998), 82.

2. It is the same reason that the Israelites were afraid to be carried off onto Babylonian lands: they were afraid that they might not find God in other places. One of the reasons why the concept of monotheism arises in the Hebrew Bible is that the Israelites experience a surprising grace when they are exiled to Babylon. There they find that the God Yahweh whom they had worshiped in the land of Israel also holds status and power to intervene and help them in a so-called foreign land.

3. Loren B. Mead, *The Once and Future Church: Reinventing the Congregation for a New Mission Frontier* (Washington, D.C.: Alban Institute, 1991).

4. See Eddie Gibbs and Ryan K. Bolger. *Emerging Churches: Creating Christian Community in Postmodern Cultures* (Grand Rapids: Baker Academic, 2005).

CHAPTER 4

1. See Stephen C. Compton, *Rekindling the Mainline: New Life though New Churches* (Bethesda, Md.: Alban Institute, 2003).

CHAPTER 5

1. Laurene Beth Bowers, "Acting-out and the Dynamics of Victimization," *Journal of Pastoral Psychology* (Sept. 1990).

2. See Eddie Gibbs and Ryan K. Bolger, *Emerging Churches: Creating Christian Community in Postmodern Cultures* (Grand Rapids: Baker Books, 2005).

3. Anthony B. Robinson, *Leadership for Vital Congregations* (Cleveland: Pilgrim Press, 2006), 33.

CHAPTER 7

1. See Eddie Gibbs and Ryan K. Bolger, *Emerging Churches: Creating Christian Community in Postmodern Cultures* (Grand Rapids: Baker Books, 2005).

2. James Thwaites, *The Church Beyond the Congregation: The Strategic Role of the Church in the Postmodern Era.* Carlisle, Cumbria, U.K.: Paternoster Press, 1999.

3. C. Kirk Hadaway and David A. Roozen, *Rerouting the Protestant Mainstream: Sources of Growth & Opportunities for Change* (Nashville: Abingdon Press, 1995).

CONCLUSION

1. E. Stanley Ott, *Twelve Dynamic Shifts for Transforming Your Church* (Grand Rapids: William B. Eerdmans, 2002), 6.

bibliography

Alston, Wallace M. *The Church of the Living God: A Reformed Perspective.* Louisville: Westminster John Knox Press, 2002.

Bandy, Thomas G. *Kicking Habits: Welcome Relief for Addicted Churches.* Nashville: Abingdon Press, 1997.

————————. *Roadrunner: The Body in Motion.* Nashville, Abingdon Press, 2002.

————————. *Moving Off the Map: A Field Guide to Changing the Congregation.* Nashville: Abingdon Press, 1998.

Bass, Diana Butler. *The Practicing Congregation: Imagining a New Old Church.* Herndon, Va.: Alban Institute, 2004.

Beckwith, Ivy. *Postmodern Children's Ministry: Ministry to Children in the 21st Century.* Grand Rapids: Zondervan. 2004.

Bowers, Laurene Beth. *Becoming a Multicultural Church.* Cleveland: Pilgrim Press, 2006.

Chesnut, Robert A. *Transforming the Mainline Church.* Louisville: Geneva Press. 2000.

Cobb, John B., Jr. *Reclaiming the Church: Where the Mainline Church Went Wrong and What to Do about It.* Louisville: Westminster John Knox Press, 1997.

Cole, Neil. *Organic Church: Growing Faith Where Life Happens.* San Francisco: Jossey-Bass, 2005.

Compton, Stephen C. *Rekindling the Mainline: New Life through New Churches.* Bethesda, Md.: Alban Institute, 2003.

Easum, William M., and Thomas G. Bandy. *Growing Spiritual Redwoods.* Nashville: Abingdon Press, 1997.

Easum, Bill, and Dave Travis. *Beyond the Box: Innovative Churches That Work.* Loveland, Colo.: Group Publishing, 2003.

Foss, Michael W. *Power Surge: Six Marks of Discipleship for a Changing Church.* Minneapolis: Fortress Press, 2000.

Gibbs, Eddie. *ChurchNext: Quantum Changes in How We Do Ministry.* Downers Grove, Ill.: Intervarsity Press, 2000.

Gibbs, Eddie, and Ryan K. Bolger. *Emerging Churches: Creating Christian Community in Postmodern Cultures.* Grand Rapids: Baker Academic, 2005.

Goodwin, Steven. J. *Catching the Next Wave: Leadership Strategies for Turn-Around Congregations.* Minneapolis: Augsburg Press, 1999.

Groff, Kent Ira. *The Soul of Tomorrow's Church: Weaving Spiritual Practices in Ministry Together.* Nashville: Upper Room Books, 2000.

Hadaway, C. Kirk, and David A. Roozen, *Rerouting the Protestant Mainstream: Sources of Growth & Opportunities for Change*. Nashville: Abingdon Press, 1995.

Jinkins, Michael. *The Church Faces Death: Ecclesiology in a Post-Modern Context*. New York: Oxford University Press, 1999.

Laubach, David. C. *Twelve Steps to Congregational Transformation: A Practical Guide for Leaders*. Valley Forge, Pa.: Judson Press, 2006.

McLaren, Brian D. *Reinventing Your Church*. Grand Rapids: Zondervan, 1998

Mead, Loren B. *New Hope for Congregations*. New York: Seabury Press, 1972.

——————. *The Once and Future Church: Reinventing the Congregation for a New Mission Frontier*. Washington, D.C.: Alban Institute, 1991.

Middleton, J. Richard, and Brian J. Walsh. *Truth is Stranger Than It Used to Be: Biblical Faith in a Postmodern Age*. Downers Grove, Ill.: Intervarsity Press, 1995.

Moynagh, Michael. *emergingchurch.intro*. Oxford, U.K.: Monarch Books, 2004.

Ott, E. Stanley. *Twelve Dynamic Shifts For Transforming Your Church*. Grand Rapids: William B. Eerdmans, 2002.

Pocock, Michael, and Joseph Henriques. *Cultural Change and Your Church*. Grand Rapids: Baker Books, 2002.

Robinson, Anthony B. *Leadership for Vital Congregations*. Cleveland: Pilgrim Press, 2006.

Rusaw, Rick, and Eric Swanson. *The Externally Focused Church*. Loveland, Colo.: Group Publishing, 2004.

Sample, Tex. *The Spectacle of Worship in a Wired World: Electronic Culture and the People of God*. Nashville: Abingdon Press, 1998.

Schaller, Lyle E. *A Mainline Turnaround: Strategies for Congregations and Denominations*. Nashville: Abingdon Press, 2005.

Steinke, Peter L. *How Your Church Family Works: Understanding Congregations as Emotional Systems*. Washington, D.C.: Alban Institute, 1993.

Thistlethwaite, Susan Brooks. *Metaphors for the Contemporary Church*. New York: Pilgrim Press, 1983.

Thwaites, James. *The Church Beyond the Congregation: The Strategic Role of the Church in the Postmodern Era*. Carlisle, Cumbria, U.K.: Paternoster Press, 1999.

Towns, Elmer, and Warren Bird. *Into the Future: Turning Today's Church Trends into Tomorrow's Opportunities*. Grand Rapids: Fleming Revell, 2000.

Warren, Rick. *The Purpose-Driven Church: Growth without Compromising Your Message & Mission*. Grand Rapids: Zondervan, 1995.

Williamson, Clark M., and Ronald J. Allen. *The Vital Church: Teaching, Worship, Community, Service*. St. Louis: Chalice Press, 1998.